The
Wiersbe
BIBLE STUDY SERIES

The Wiersbe

BIBLE STUDY SERIES

MINOR PROPHETS
VOLUME 3

Making a

Difference

in Your

Lifetime

David C Cook®

transforming lives together

THE WIERSBE BIBLE STUDY SERIES: MINOR PROPHETS (VOLUME 3)
Published by David C Cook
4050 Lee Vance View
Colorado Springs, CO 80918 U.S.A.

David C Cook Distribution Canada
55 Woodslee Avenue, Paris, Ontario, Canada N3L 3E5

David C Cook U.K., Kingsway Communications
Eastbourne, East Sussex BN23 6NT, England

The graphic circle C logo is a registered trademark of David C Cook.

All excerpts taken from *Be Concerned*, second edition, published by David C
Cook in 2010 © 1996 Warren W. Wiersbe, ISBN 978-0-7814-0337-5.

ISBN 978-0-7814-1040-3

eISBN 978-1-4347-0929-5
© 2015 Warren W. Wiersbe

The Team: Steve Parolini, Karen Lee-Thorpe, Jack Campbell, Amy
Konyndyk, Nick Lee, Karen Athen, Channing Brooks

Series Cover Design: John Hamilton Design
Cover Photo: [to come]
Printed in the United States of America

First Edition 2015

1 2 3 4 5 6 7 8 9 10

042315

Contents

Introduction to Minor Prophets (Volume 3)

Not So Minor

Amos, Obadiah, Micah, and Zephaniah may be "minor" prophets in the lengths of their books, as compared to Isaiah, Jeremiah, and Ezekiel, but they certainly aren't minor in their messages. These men dealt courageously with the sins of God's people, warning them that chastening judgments would come if the people didn't repent and turn to God. But they were also tenderhearted in their messages of forgiveness and hope.

In the words of Paul, these prophets proclaimed "the kindness and sternness of God" (Rom. 11:22), a balanced message that we need to hear today.

The Company of the Concerned

In our pluralistic society, some preachers and teachers try so hard to be politically correct that they end up with no message at all, while others do not understand the mind-set of their hearers and fail to get through. The prophets made neither mistake, and we can learn from them how best to declare God's truth.

Having heard these messages, we need to act on them and obey what God tells us to do. The great need of the hour is for "the company of the concerned" to follow Christ and accomplish His will in this needy world.

—*Warren W. Wiersbe*

How to Use This Study

This study is designed for both individual and small-group use. We've divided it into eight lessons—each references one or more chapters in Warren W. Wiersbe's commentary *Be Concerned* (second edition, David C Cook, 2010). While reading *Be Concerned* is not a prerequisite for going through this study, the additional insights and background Wiersbe offers can greatly enhance your study experience.

The **Getting Started** questions at the beginning of each lesson offer you an opportunity to record your first thoughts and reactions to the study text. This is an important step in the study process as those "first impressions" often include clues about what it is your heart is longing to discover.

The bulk of the study is found in the **Going Deeper** questions. These dive into the Bible text and, along with helpful excerpts from Wiersbe's commentary, help you examine not only the original context and meaning of the verses but also modern application.

Looking Inward narrows the focus down to your personal story. These intimate questions can be a bit uncomfortable at times, but don't shy away from honesty here. This is where you are asked to stand before the mirror of God's Word and look closely at what you see. It's the place to take a good look at yourself in light of the lesson and search for ways in which you can grow in faith.

Going Forward is the place where you can commit to paper those things you want or need to do in order to better live out the discoveries you made in the Looking Inward section. Don't skip or skim through this. Take the time to really consider what practical steps you might take to move closer to Christ. Then share your thoughts with a trusted friend who can act as an encourager and accountability partner.

Finally, there is a brief **Seeking Help** section to close the lesson. This is a reminder for you to invite God into your spiritual-growth process. If you choose to write out a prayer in this section, come back to it as you work through the lesson and continue to seek the Holy Spirit's guidance as you discover God's will for your life.

Tips for Small Groups

A small group is a dynamic thing. One week it might seem like a group of close-knit friends. The next it might seem more like a group of uncomfortable strangers. A small-group leader's role is to read these subtle changes and adjust the tone of the discussion accordingly.

Small groups need to be safe places for people to talk openly. It is through shared wrestling with difficult life issues that some of the greatest personal growth is discovered. But in order for the group to feel safe, participants need to know it's okay *not* to share sometimes. Always invite honest disclosure, but never force someone to speak if he or she isn't comfortable doing so. (A savvy leader will follow up later with a group member who isn't comfortable sharing in a group setting to see if a one-on-one discussion is more appropriate.)

Have volunteers take turns reading excerpts from Scripture or from the commentary. The more each person is involved even in the mundane tasks, the more they'll feel comfortable opening up in more meaningful ways.

The leader should watch the clock and keep the discussion moving. Sometimes there may be more Going Deeper questions than your group can cover in your available time. If you've had a fruitful discussion, it's okay to move on without finishing everything. And if you think the group is getting bogged down on a question or has taken off on a tangent, you can simply say, "Let's go on to question 5." Be sure to save at least ten to fifteen minutes for the Going Forward questions.

Finally, soak your group meetings in prayer—before you begin, during as needed, and always at the end of your time together.

The Lion
(AMOS I—2)

Before you begin …
- *Pray for the Holy Spirit to reveal truth and wisdom as you go through this lesson.*
- *Read Amos 1—2. This lesson references chapter 1 in* Be Concerned. *It will be helpful for you to have your Bible and a copy of the commentary available as you work through this lesson.*

Getting Started

From the Commentary

Amos ("burden bearer") was a herdsman and a cultivator of sycamore trees (Amos 1:1; 7:14) when the Lord called him to be a prophet. He lived in the village of Tekoa, about eleven miles from Jerusalem, during the reigns of Uzziah in Judah (790–740 BC) and Jeroboam II in the northern kingdom of Israel (793–753). Amos was a layman, a humble farmer and shepherd who was not an official member of the Jewish religious or political establishment.

—*Be Concerned*, page 13

1. What is significant about Amos's profession prior to his call to prophesy? What does this tell us about how God chooses His prophets? What does it teach us about how God can use "common" people even today?

2. Choose one verse or phrase from Amos 1—2 that stands out to you. This could be something you're intrigued by, something that makes you uncomfortable, something that puzzles you, something that resonates with you, or just something you want to examine further. Write that here.

Going Deeper

From the Commentary

If the prophet Amos were to come to our world today, he would probably feel very much at home; for he lived at a time such as ours, when society was changing radically. Both Israel and Judah were at peace with their neighbors, which meant that their wealth and energy could be used for developing their nations instead of fighting their enemies. Both kingdoms were prosperous; their cities were expanding rapidly; and a new wealthy merchant class was developing in society. The two kingdoms were moving from an agricultural to a commercial society and experiencing both the benefits and problems that come with that change.

However, in spite of their material success, all was not well with God's chosen people.

—*Be Concerned*, page 15

3. What were some of the ills God's people were experiencing? What unpopular message did Amos give God's people? What sort of message might they have been expecting from God? What does this teach us about how God gets right to the heart of the matter?

More to Consider: Nothing would have made the Jews happier than to see the Lord judge the surrounding nations. But when Amos denounced Judah and Israel, that was a different story. How do believers today sometimes take a similar attitude toward God's judgment?

From the Commentary

God wanted to get the nations' attention, but people weren't listening. You'd think they could hear a lion roar or the thunder roll and know that danger was at hand. God was speaking ("thundering") from Jerusalem, for judgment always begins at the house of the Lord (1 Peter 4:17). He had sent drought to the land so that even fruitful Carmel was withering, but it didn't bring the people to their knees. So God called a common farmer to preach to His people and warn them. "A lion has roared! Who will not fear? The Lord GOD has spoken! Who can but prophesy?" (Amos 3:8 NKJV).

Eight times Amos used the phrase "for three transgressions and for four," a Jewish idiom that means "an indefinite number that has finally come to the end."

—*Be Concerned*, page 16

4. Review Amos 1:3, 6, 9, 11, and 13. In what ways does God exercise longsuffering with sinners? (See 2 Peter 3:9.) Does His patience run out? Explain. In what ways is testing God's patience similar to tempting God?

From Today's World

The news is rife with stories clamoring for our attention—everything from natural disasters to the sins of the famous to the imminent threat of war. A day doesn't go by without something "big" being shouted as breaking news on our televisions and our computer screens. In Old Testament times, of course, there were no 24-7 news outlets shouting the latest thing to be concerned about or to celebrate. Instead, news traveled from ear to ear. When God spoke through the prophets, His voice sounded like that of a man. It might have been easy to dismiss Amos and his ilk as crazy people who claimed to speak for God. But the truth of their words proved God's voice. Today, however, with so many people shouting, and an apparent dearth of traditional prophets, it's harder than ever to hear God.

5. Where do today's believers hear God's voice? How do they know when they're hearing from God and not just from people (crazy or otherwise)? What tools do we have today to help us sort through the noise of breaking news to hear the voice of God?

From the Commentary

> The phrase "I will send a fire" (Amos 1:4, 7, 10, 12, 14; 2:2, 5) means "I will send judgment"; for fire represents the holiness and judgment of God (Deut. 4:11, 24,

36; Heb. 12:29). Indeed, the Lord did judge Syria: the dynasty of King Hazael ended; his son Ben-Hadad was defeated; Damascus lost its power (business was done at the city gate, Amos 1:5); and "the house of Eden" (delight, paradise) became a ruin. King Josiah defeated Ben-Hadad three times (2 Kings 13:25), but it was the Assyrians who finally subdued Syria and took them into captivity.

—*Be Concerned*, page 17

6. What is it about fire that makes it a fitting image of judgment? How is that imagery reframed in the New Testament (Matt. 3:7–12; 1 Cor. 3:10–15)? What does fire represent in the redemption story?

From the Commentary

During the reigns of David and Solomon, Israel had a warm relationship with the people of Tyre (1 Kings 5:1ff.). Amos called it "the brotherly covenant" ("treaty of broth-erhood" NIV), suggesting that the "covenant" was more than a treaty but involved a friendly partnership that went deeper than politics. Even if the peoples of different nations don't agree in their religious practices or their political structures, they can still treat one another like fellow human beings.

Tyre, however, committed the same sins as the Philistine cities by selling Jewish captives to the Edomites as slaves (Amos 1:6–8). When the prophet Ezekiel gave his funeral dirge celebrating the fall of Tyre, he mentioned this grievous sin (Ezek. 27:13). But Tyre's sin was worse than that of Philistia because Tyre was violating a long-standing compact that was based on friendship and mutual respect for humanity. Tyre was selling its friends as slaves!

Judgment came in 332 BC when Alexander the Great wiped Tyre off the face of the earth and left it a place for drying nets (Ezek. 26:5, 14).

—*Be Concerned*, page 18

7. Review Amos 1:9–10. Why is it notable that Tyre was given such harsh judgment, even though it was once an ally? What does this reveal about God's ongoing judgment of the world? What does it teach us about God's sovereignty?

From the Commentary

> The Edomites would not allow their Jewish cousins to pass through their land during Israel's march to Canaan (Num. 20:14–21). King Saul suppressed the Edomite army (1 Sam. 14:47), and David conquered them (2 Sam. 8:14), but in the days of King Jehoram, Edom revolted against Judah and won their freedom (2 Kings 8:16–22).
>
> Amos condemned the Edomites for their persistent hatred of the Jews, "because his anger raged continually and his fury flamed unchecked" (Amos 1:11 NIV). We don't know when the Edomites aided the enemy by pursuing the Jews with the sword. It could have been during any one of the numerous times when enemies invaded the land. When the Babylonians attacked and captured Jerusalem, the Edomites assisted the enemy and gave vent to their anger (Obad. 10–14; see Ps. 137:7). You would think that brother would help brother in a time of need, but the Edomites "cast off all pity" (Amos 1:11) and acted like beasts instead of humans. The phrase "his anger did tear" (v. 11) uses a verb that describes ferocious beasts tearing their prey (Ps. 7:2; Gen. 37:33).
>
> *—Be Concerned*, page 19

8. Why did the Edomites despise their Jewish cousins? (See the story of Jacob and Esau in Genesis 25:27–34, 27:1–41, and Hebrews 12:16–17.) Why are there so many biblical accounts of enmity between brothers? In

what ways does this sort of familial dissension or disagreement affect the modern church?

More to Consider: The Edomites lived "in the clefts of the rocks" and had their "nest among the stars" (Obad. 3–4), boasting that their fortresses were impregnable. Why is this significant in light of God's judgment? What does it say about God's judgment that there is nothing left today except ruins?

From the Commentary

In his six messages, Amos had announced judgment to the nations surrounding Israel and Judah, starting with Syria in the northwest and ending with the trans-Jordanic nations of Ammon, Moab, and Edom. (There's probably a map of the divided kingdom in the back of your Bible.) As his fellow Jews heard these denunciations of the Gentiles, no doubt they applauded and wanted to hear more. But when Amos focused on Israel and Judah (his own land), that changed their attitude completely. The very idea of a

Jewish prophet classifying God's chosen people with the Gentile "dogs"! "We know we aren't a perfect people," the people of Judah would argue, "but at least we worship the true and living God!"

Yes, the temple was filled with people bringing their sacrifices, but Judah was a nation given over to idolatry. "Their lies [idols] lead them astray, lies which their fathers followed" (Amos 2:4 NKJV). They were wandering like lost animals and like drunken men. The Gentiles had sinned against conscience and the laws of brotherhood and humanity, but the Jews had despised and rejected the very laws of God, given to them by Moses. Theirs was the greater sin, for greater privilege always brings greater responsibility (Rom. 2:17—3:9).

—*Be Concerned*, pages 21–22

9. Review Amos 2:4–5. How was this judgment different from past judgments against God's people? What's significant about the fact that God would judge them out of their land? In what ways was the threat of being taken captive by the Babylonians a more severe judgment than being invaded by other nations?

From the Commentary

Both Israel and Judah were enjoying peace and prosperity, and divine judgment was the furthest thing from their minds. Remember, Jewish theology equated prosperity with God's blessing; and as long as the people were enjoying "the good life," they were sure God was pleased with them. They knew what the law said about their sins, but they chose to ignore the warnings.

Amos first exposes *their sinful present* and names three flagrant sins. To begin with, the people of the northern kingdom were guilty of *injustice* (Amos 2:6–7). Supported by corrupt judges, the rich were suing the poor, who couldn't pay their bills, and forcing them into servitude and slavery. Even if they couldn't pay for a pair of shoes, the poor were neither forgiven nor assisted. Instead, they were trampled like the dust of the earth. As we shall see in our continued studies, the prophet Amos has a great deal to say about caring for the poor (see 4:1; 5:11; 8:6; also Deut. 15:7–11; Ex. 23:6–9; Prov. 14:31; 17:15).

Their second gross sin was *immorality* (Amos 2:7b), with fathers and sons visiting the same prostitute! These may have been "cult prostitutes" who were a part of the heathen idolatrous worship. Thus there was a double sin involved: immorality and idolatry. Or the girl may have been a household servant or a common prostitute. You would think that a father would want to be a better example to his son by obeying the law of Moses (Ex. 22:16; Deut. 22:28–29; 23:17–18). Perhaps what's described here is a form of incest, which was, of course, strictly forbidden by Moses (Lev. 18:7–8, 15; 20:11–12). Regardless of what the act of disobedience was, it was rebellion against God and defiled His holy name.

The third sin was *open idolatry* (Amos 2:8). Wealthy men took their debtors' garments as pledges but did not return them at sundown as the law commanded (Ex. 22:26–27; Deut. 24:10–13, 17). Instead, these rich sinners visited pagan altars, where they got drunk on wine purchased with the fines they exacted from the poor. Then, in their drunken stupor, they slept by the altars on other people's garments, defiling the garments and disobeying the law. The officials were getting rich by exploiting the people, and then were using their unjust gain for committing sin.

After describing their sinful present, Amos reminded them of *their glorious past* (Amos 2:9–12).

—*Be Concerned*, pages 22–24

10. Review Amos 2:6–16. Why were these three sins singled out? What do they reveal about God's heart? Why did Amos then remind the people of their glorious past (2:9–12)? How did remembering the "good old days" help the Jews understand God's judgment?

Looking Inward

Take a moment to reflect on all that you've explored thus far in this study of Amos 1—2. Review your notes and answers and think about how each of these things matters in your life today.

Tips for Small Groups: To get the most out of this section, form pairs or trios and have group members take turns answering these questions. Be honest and as open as you can in this discussion, but most of all, be encouraging and supportive of others. Be sensitive to those who are going through particularly difficult times and don't press for people to speak if they're uncomfortable doing so.

11. How would you respond if God called you to be a prophet today? What would you fear most? How would you approach the idea of telling the world potentially unsettling news?

12. How do you know when someone is speaking for God and when that person is speaking for just himself or herself? What are the tests you use to verify God's voice in a matter?

13. How do messages of God's judgment affect you? Are they frightening? Familiar and therefore without much impact? Do you take them to heart or think of them as applying to someone else? How easy is it for you to want to worship a God of judgment?

Going Forward

14. Think of one or two things that you have learned that you'd like to work on in the coming week. Remember that this is all about quality, not quantity. It's better to work on one specific area of life and do it well than to work on many and do poorly (or to be so overwhelmed that you simply don't try).

Do you want to learn how to better hear God's voice? Be specific. Go back through Amos 1—2 and put a star next to the phrase or verse that is most encouraging to you. Consider memorizing this verse.

Real-Life Application Ideas: Hold an "interview for modern prophets" with your small group. During this event, discuss the excitement and fears that would come from being called by God to speak to His people. Make it a fun event, but don't miss out on the bigger significance of what it means to be called by God. Then spend some time discussing what it means to serve God right where you are. What are some ways you each have been called by God to deliver a message to the world, or at least to your local community?

Seeking Help

15. Write a prayer below (or simply pray one in silence), inviting God to work on your mind and heart in those areas you've noted in the Going Forward section. Be honest about your desires and fears.

Notes for Small Groups:

- *Look for ways to put into practice the things you wrote in the Going Forward section. Talk with other group members about your ideas and commit to being accountable to one another.*

- *During the coming week, ask the Holy Spirit to continue to reveal truth to you from what you've read and studied.*

- *Before you start the next lesson, read Amos 3—4. For more in-depth lesson preparation, read chapters 2 and 3, "Listen to What God Says" and "Sins in Good Standing," in* Be Concerned.

What God Says
(AMOS 3—4)

Before you begin …
- *Pray for the Holy Spirit to reveal truth and wisdom as you go through this lesson.*
- *Read Amos 3—4. This lesson references chapters 2 and 3 in* Be Concerned. *It will be helpful for you to have your Bible and a copy of the commentary available as you work through this lesson.*

Getting Started

From the Commentary

Now that Amos had the attention of the people, he proceeded to deliver three messages, each of which begins with "Hear this word" (3:1; 4:1; 5:1). By using this phrase, he reminded them that they weren't listening to a mere man making a speech; they were listening to a prophet declaring the living word of God.

It's indeed a great privilege to have God speak to us, but it's also a great responsibility. If we don't open our hearts to hear His Word and obey Him, we're in grave danger of hardening our hearts and incurring the wrath of God. "Today, if you will hear His voice, do not harden your hearts" (Heb. 3:7–8 NKJV; see Ps. 95:7–11).

The first message (Amos 3) was one of *explanation*, in which Amos clarified four divine calls and announced that Israel's judgment was certain. His second message (Amos 4) focused on *accusation*, in which the prophet denounced Israel's sins. The final message (Amos 5:1—6:14) was a *lamentation* as the prophet felt the anguish of his nation's certain doom.

—*Be Concerned*, page 29

1. What's the connection between being chosen and being disciplined in Amos 3:2? How might the Jews have seen this as a surprising connection? Are chosenness and discipline still connected in that way? Explain.

2. Choose one verse or phrase from Amos 3—4 that stands out to you. This could be something you're intrigued by, something that makes you

uncomfortable, something that puzzles you, something that resonates with you, or just something you want to examine further. Write that here.

Going Deeper

From the Commentary

> The message in Amos 3:1–2 was delivered to "the whole family," that is, to both Israel and Judah; for both kingdoms were guilty of disobeying God's holy law. Amos reminded them of their divine calling as the people of God, a calling that they were prone to despise and forget.
>
> What kind of a calling did God give to the Jewish nation? To begin with, it was a *gracious call*; for the Lord had chosen them and no other nation to be the special recipients of His bountiful gifts. "For you are a holy people to the Lord your God; the Lord your God has chosen you to be a people for Himself, a special treasure above all the peoples on the face of the earth. The Lord did not set His love on you nor choose you because you were more in number than any other people, for you were the least of all peoples; but because the Lord loves you, and because He would keep the oath which He swore to your fathers" (Deut. 7:6–8 NKJV; see Ex. 19:1–5).
>
> —*Be Concerned*, page 30

3. How was God's call a gracious call? What does this say about His relationship with His people at this time in history? How does this principle of "gracious election" apply to the church? (See John 15:16; 1 Cor. 1:26–29; Eph. 1:13–14.)

More to Consider: How might some people mistake the doctrine of divine election as an excuse to sin? How is divine election supposed to inspire and change us? (See 1 John 3:1–2.) In what ways does privilege always come with responsibility? (See John 15:16; Eph. 1:3–5; 1 Peter 2:4–5, 9.)

From the Commentary

At this point, the people were probably saying, "Who is this rustic farmer that he should preach to us and claim to be God's prophet? What kind of authority does he think he has?" Amos even dared to preach uninvited at the king's chapel at Bethel, where King Jeroboam's chaplain told Amos to go home and preach in Judah (Amos 7:10–16).

No doubt when D. L. Moody began to preach, some people said, "What can this uneducated shoe salesman say to us?" And when Billy Sunday began to hold evangelistic campaigns, it's likely that the sophisticated religious crowd asked, "What can this former baseball player teach us?" But God used Moody and Sunday, not in spite of their humble background, but because of it; for He delights to bypass the "wise and prudent" and share His power with "babes" (Luke 10:21).

Now for the final thrust: If an untrained rustic farmer is preaching God's Word, *it means God has called him.* This isn't a vocation Amos would have chosen for himself; it was chosen for him by the Lord. Amos said, "I was neither a prophet nor a prophet's son, but I was a shepherd, and I also took care of sycamore-fig trees. But the LORD took me from tending the flock and said to me, 'Go, prophesy to my people Israel'" (Amos 7:14–15 NIV).

When a prophet proclaims God's Word, it's because the Lord is about to do something important and wants to warn His people (3:7).

—*Be Concerned*, pages 31–32

4. Review Amos 3:3–8. How would these words have been an effective response to people ridiculing the idea that God had sent Amos to prophesy judgment? What lesson is there in the prophet's reply for how Christians today can deal with disdain or ridicule?

From the Commentary

In his day, the prophet Isaiah called heaven and earth to witness against Judah (Isa. 1:2; see Deut. 30:19; 31:28); and Amos summoned the Gentile nations to witness against the northern kingdom of Israel, whose capital was Samaria. The sin of Israel was so great that it even appalled the pagan nations; for, after all, Israel was sinning against a flood of light (1 Cor. 5:1).

It's tragic and humiliating when the unsaved world catches professed Christians in their sins. It happened to Abraham twice when he lied to heathen kings about his wife, Sarah (Gen. 12:10–20; 20:1ff.). Samson was shamed before the Philistines (Judg. 16), and David was embarrassed before the king of Gath (1 Sam. 21:10–15). David's adultery with Bathsheba gave "great occasion to the enemies of the LORD to blaspheme" (2 Sam. 12:14). In the late 1980s, the media ministry scandals brought great shame to the church; and whenever a prominent servant of God falls into sin, the news media seem to enjoy telling the story.

Amos called for the Philistines ("Ashdod," Amos 1:8) and the Egyptians to witness what was going on in Samaria (v. 9). The leaders of Israel weren't interested in obeying God's law and helping the less fortunate. Rather, they were eagerly and unjustly robbing the poor and amassing as much wealth as possible. They built costly houses, filled them with expensive furnishings, and lived in luxury, while the poor of the land suffered (3:15; 4:1; 5:11; 6:4–6).

—*Be Concerned*, pages 33–34

5. Why did Amos focus on the exploitation of the poor by the rich as one of his main themes? What did the law of Moses have to say about caring for the poor? (See Ex. 22:25–27; 23:11; Lev. 19:9–15; 25:6; Deut. 14:28–29; 15:12–13; 16:11–14.) How is this message relevant today?

From the Commentary

In Amos 3:11–15, the prophet announced that the kingdom of Israel would fall to an enemy and the great city of Samaria would be plundered. This happened in 722 BC when the Assyrians invaded Israel. The people of Israel had plundered one another, but now a pagan Gentile nation would plunder them. We reap what we sow.

To illustrate what would happen to Israel, Amos borrowed from his experiences as a shepherd. According to Exodus 22:10–13, if a lion took a sheep and tore it to pieces, the shepherd had to bring the remnants of the sheep to prove that it was truly dead (see Gen. 31:39). This would assure the owner of the flock that the shepherd wasn't stealing the sheep and lying to his employer. By the time Assyria was through with Israel, only a small remnant of the people would be left. The lion was about to roar (Amos 1:2; 3:8)!

According to 2 Kings 17:5ff., the Assyrians killed some Israelites, took others captive, and then brought into the land captives from other nations, thus producing a people with diverse racial and religious backgrounds. The surviving Jews in the ten tribes of the northern kingdom married people who were not Jews, and this produced the people we know as Samaritans. The "pure" Jews rejected this new "mongrel race" (John 4:9); so the Samaritans set up their own temple and priesthood and established their own religion, which the Lord rejected (vv. 19–24).

—*Be Concerned*, pages 35–36

6. Why was it important for Amos to tell the people the Assyrian invasion was a work of God? Why was God punishing them? (See Amos 3:14.) How would you feel to hear that your nation was going to become like scraps left by a lion (3:12)?

From the Commentary

In this second message, the prophet Amos named three particular sins that were grieving the Lord and ruining the kingdom of Israel: luxury (4:1–3), hypocrisy (vv. 4–5), and obstinacy (vv. 6–13). They had the wrong values; their religious "revival" was a sham; and they had refused to listen to the warnings God had given them.

The word *luxury* comes from a Latin word that means "excessive." It originally referred to plants that grow abundantly (our English word *luxurious*), but then it came to refer to people who have an abundance of money, time, and comfort, which they use for themselves as they live in aimless leisure. Whenever you are offered "deluxe service," that's the same Latin word: service above and beyond what you really need.

—*Be Concerned*, pages 41–42

7. What was the luxury that Amos addressed in 4:1–3? Is it a sin to be rich? Why or why not? Respond to this in light of Amos's message: Luxury doesn't mean owning abundant possessions so much as allowing possessions to own us.

From the Commentary

The prophet used "holy irony" in Amos 4:4–5, for he later instructed the people to do just the opposite (Amos 5:5).

It's as though a pastor today said to his congregation, "Sure, go ahead and attend church, but by attending, you're only sinning more. Go and visit the summer Bible conferences, but by doing so, you will be transgressing more. Your heart isn't serious about knowing God or doing His will. It's all just playacting; it's the popular thing to do, so you do it."

Bethel was a very special place to the Jewish people because of its associations with Abraham (Gen. 12:8; 13:3) and Jacob (28:10–22; 35:1–7). At one time, the ark was kept at Bethel (Judg. 20:18–28), but in Amos's day it was the site of "the king's chapel," where Amaziah, the priest, served (Amos 7:10ff.). Gilgal was also important to Israel because that's where Joshua and the people camped when they first entered the Promised Land (Josh. 4:19–20; 5:2–9). Gilgal is also where Saul was made king of Israel (1 Sam. 11:15). Unfortunately, both of these places had become shrines, where the people worshipped pagan gods while claiming to worship the Lord.

—*Be Concerned*, pages 44–45

8. On the surface, it looked as if Israel was experiencing a religious revival. Crowds of people were flocking to the "holy places," bringing their sacrifices and tithes (Amos 4:4; 5:21–22) and even singing songs of praise to the Lord (5:23; 6:5). What was really going on? How can we tell that their expression of spirituality was false? (See 5:24.) What determines whether our sacrifices are sincere?

More to Consider: The people of Israel loved going to religious meetings, but they didn't love the God they claimed to worship. Making a pilgrimage to Bethel or Gilgal was the popular thing to do in that day, and everybody wanted to keep up with the crowd. There was no confession of sin or brokenness before the Lord, but only a religious event that made the participants feel good. What are some parallels in the modern church to what the Jews were doing in Amos's time? Why is the appearance of spirituality tempting to put on? What does it accomplish?

From the Commentary

The people in Amos's day didn't return home determined to help the poor, feed the hungry, and care for the widows and orphans. They went home with the same selfish hearts that they had when they left home, because their "worship" was only an empty ritual (Isa. 1:11–17). Any religious "revival" that doesn't alter the priorities of Christians and help solve the problems in society isn't a revival at all.

It's interesting that Amos mentioned music, because that's an important part of the church's worship.

—*Be Concerned*, page 46

9. Why might God have called the Jews' beautiful music "noise" (Amos 5:23)? What makes music today pleasing to God? What makes it "noise"? Why is that distinction important in the life of the church?

From the Commentary

> Five times in Amos 4:6–13, the prophet says to the peo-
> ple, "Yet you have not returned to Me" (4:6, 8, 9, 10, 11
> NKJV). The people of Israel experienced God's discipline,
> but they wouldn't submit to His will; and yet they contin-
> ued practicing their hypocritical religion! "Not everyone
> who says to Me, 'Lord, Lord,' shall enter the kingdom of
> heaven, but he who does the will of My Father in heaven"
> (Matt. 7:21 NKJV).
>
> God's covenant with the Jews clearly stated that He
> would bless them if they obeyed His law and would dis-
> cipline them if they disobeyed (Deut. 27—29). God set
> before them life and death, blessing and cursing; and He
> urged them to choose life (30:19–20). Unfortunately,
> they spurned His love, rejected His warnings, and chose
> death.
>
> Consider some of the disciplines that God sent to Israel to
> bring His people back to Himself.
>
> —*Be Concerned*, page 47

10. What were some of the disciplines God sent to Israel to bring His
people back to Him (Amos 4:6–11)? How should each of these have drawn
the people back to Him? Why didn't the effect last? How did Amos end
this message (4:13)? What does the ability to praise God in the midst of
trials say about those who do that?

Looking Inward

Take a moment to reflect on all that you've explored thus far in this study of Amos 3—4. Review your notes and answers and think about how each of these things matters in your life today.

Tips for Small Groups: To get the most out of this section, form pairs or trios and have group members take turns answering these questions. Be honest and as open as you can in this discussion, but most of all, be encouraging and supportive of others. Be sensitive to those who are going through particularly difficult times and don't press for people to speak if they're uncomfortable doing so.

11. Have you ever been picked on or ridiculed for standing up for your faith or sharing God's truth with someone? If so, describe that experience. What was your response? How did your faith in God help you deal with that kind of negative attention?

12. What does luxury mean to you? Have you ever been tempted to pursue money and possessions in an unhealthy way? What prompted that temptation? Why is it often hard to trust God to care for us when things are difficult? Why is it so important to do this?

13. What kind of music do you consider to be worshipful? Have you ever been in a church service where the music was nothing more than "noise" as Amos described it? How important is it to bring a humble heart to a worship service, whether you're leading it or participating in it?

Going Forward

14. Think of one or two things that you have learned that you'd like to work on in the coming week. Remember that this is all about quality, not quantity. It's better to work on one specific area of life and do it well than to work on many and do poorly (or to be so overwhelmed that you simply don't try).

Do you want to truly worship rather than just make "noise"? Be specific. Go back through Amos 3—4 and put a star next to the phrase or verse that is most encouraging to you. Consider memorizing this verse.

Real-Life Application Ideas: Hold a family (or small-group) worship service. But instead of filling the time with song, spend the first half of your time in prayer (both private and corporate), asking God to prepare your heart and the hearts of your family or group members for a time of shared singing and praising God. The most important aspect of worship is the heart you bring to it, not the act itself. Then use this model of preparing your heart every time you attend a worship service.

Seeking Help

15. Write a prayer below (or simply pray one in silence), inviting God to work on your mind and heart in those areas you've noted in the Going Forward section. Be honest about your desires and fears.

Notes for Small Groups:

- *Look for ways to put into practice the things you wrote in the Going Forward section. Talk with other group members about your ideas and commit to being accountable to one another.*

- *During the coming week, ask the Holy Spirit to continue to reveal truth to you from what you've read and studied.*

- *Before you start the next lesson, read Amos 5—6. For more in-depth lesson preparation, read chapters 4 and 5, "How to Avoid the Storm" and "'Woe to the Sinners!'" in* Be Concerned.

Avoiding the Storm
(AMOS 5—6)

Before you begin …
- *Pray for the Holy Spirit to reveal truth and wisdom as you go through this lesson.*
- *Read Amos 5—6. This lesson references chapters 4 and 5 in* Be Concerned. *It will be helpful for you to have your Bible and a copy of the commentary available as you work through this lesson.*

Getting Started

From the Commentary

The prophet's third message (Amos 5:1—6:14) was a lamentation, a funeral dirge over the death of the nation of Israel. (Israel is mentioned four times in 5:1–4.) "There will be wailing in all the streets," he declares (v. 16 NIV), not just wailing in one or two houses where people have died. Since the people's grief will be so great that there won't be sufficient professional mourners available to express it, they'll call the farmers and workers in the vineyards to help them (vv. 16–17).

However, Amos weaves into his lamentation three pleas to the people, urging them to return to the Lord.

The first plea (5:1–3) is "Hear God's Word." This is the third time Amos has called the people to give attention to God's Word (3:1; 4:1). The way we treat God's Word is the way we treat God, and the way we treat God's messengers is the way we treat the Lord Himself (John 15:18–21). "God ... has in these last days spoken to us by His Son.... See that you do not refuse Him who speaks" (Heb. 1:1–2; 12:25 NKJV).

—*Be Concerned*, page 53

1. Why would the people have been perplexed about Amos's grieving over the death of his nation? Why did Amos compare the nation to a dead virgin? How do you think the people received that description? Why were God's people so often slow to hear the truth beneath the words prophets spoke on God's behalf? What keeps us from hearing God's truth today?

More to Consider: The first step toward revival and returning to the Lord is to hear what God has to say to us from His Word. "Will you not revive us again, that your people may rejoice in you? Show us your unfailing love, O LORD, and grant us your salvation. I will listen to what God the LORD will say; he promises peace to his people, his saints— but let them not return to folly" (Ps. 85:6–8). What does it mean that God "promises peace to his people, his saints"? How did this apply to the Israelites in Amos's time? Why did they struggle to hear God?

2. Choose one verse or phrase from Amos 5—6 that stands out to you. This could be something you're intrigued by, something that makes you uncomfortable, something that puzzles you, something that resonates with you, or just something you want to examine further. Write that here.

Going Deeper

From the Commentary

The phrase "seek the LORD" (Amos 5:6) is found more than thirty times in Scripture. It applied to Israel in ancient days, and it applies to God's children today. Even if the whole nation (or church) doesn't respond to the message and return to the Lord, a remnant can return and receive the

Lord's help and blessing. God was willing to save the evil
city of Sodom if He had found ten righteous people in it
(Gen. 18:32); and in Jeremiah's day, the Lord would have
been happy to find even one righteous person in Jerusalem!
God can work through the many or the few (1 Sam. 14:6);
we should never despise the day of small things (Zech. 4:10).

—*Be Concerned*, page 55

3. What does it mean to "seek the Lord"? (See Isa. 55:6–7.) In what ways
were the Israelites thinking wrongly about God, sin, and life? What kinds
of changes in the way we think are required in order to seek the Lord? Why
should we seek the Lord?

From the Commentary

To "seek the Lord" might appear difficult and distant for
some people, an intangible experience they can't get their
hands on. Thus Amos brought the challenge down to
practical, everyday life. He spoke about justice, righteousness, and the importance of telling the truth. He named
the sins the people needed to forsake: accepting bribes,

charging the poor exorbitant rents, living in luxury while the poor starved, and sustaining a crooked legal system. True repentance begins with naming sins and dealing with them one by one.

We must notice that Amos 5:8–9 are a parenthesis in the prophet's message, but a very important parenthesis as he reminded the people of the greatness of their God. Jehovah is the God who created the heavens and the earth, who controls the seasons and the daily motions of the earth, and who is Lord of the heavens, the sea, and the land. The pagan Gentiles worshiped the heavenly bodies, but the Jews were privileged to worship the God who made the heavens and the earth (Jonah 1:9).

But this God of creation is also the God of judgment! "He flashes destruction on the stronghold and brings the fortified city to ruin" (Amos 5:9 NIV). J. B. Phillips graphically translated verse 9, "He it is who flings ruin in the face of the strong, and rains destruction upon the fortress." In the light of the holiness of God and the terms of His holy covenant, the people of Israel should have been on their faces, calling out for mercy. Instead, they were complacently comfortable in their luxury and their sins.

—*Be Concerned,* page 58

4. Review Amos 5:7–13. What are some of the sins Amos named in this passage? How were the people promoting injustice? In what ways were they oppressing the poor? What are some injustices today that you think trouble God?

From the Commentary

Amos 5:14–15 implies that the people were boasting, "The Lord God is with us!" After all, wasn't the nation enjoying great prosperity? Certainly that was a sign of God's blessing. And weren't the people active in religious activities, bringing their sacrifices and offerings to the shrines? And didn't the king have a special priest and a royal sanctuary in Bethel (Amos 7:10–17), where he consulted with Amaziah about the affairs of the kingdom?

Yes, these things were true, but they could not be used as evidence of the blessing of God. They were but a thin veneer of religious self-righteousness over the rotting corpse of the nation. The only proof that God is with us is that we love Him and do His will. Religion without righteousness and justice in the land is hypocrisy. No matter how many people attend religious meetings, if the result is not obedience to God and concern for our neighbors, the meetings are a failure.

—*Be Concerned*, page 61

5. Why must people hate evil in order to love good? In what ways does seeking good mean rejecting evil? How were the Israelites failing at this? How do we fail at this in the modern church?

From the Commentary

"The day of the LORD" (Amos 5:18, 20) is a period of time during which God judges His enemies and establishes His kingdom on earth. It's the answer to our prayer "Thy kingdom come" and is described in Revelation 6—20 and many passages in the books of the prophets.

The people Amos was addressing saw "the day of the LORD" as a time of great deliverance for the Jews and terrible punishment for the Gentiles (Joel 2:28–32), but the prophets had a clearer vision of this momentous event. They realized that "the day of the LORD" was also a time of testing and purifying for Israel (see Isa. 2:10–21; 13:6–13; Jer. 46:10; Joel 3:9–17; Zeph. 2:1–2), when God's people would go through tribulation before entering the kingdom of God.

—*Be Concerned*, pages 65–66

6. Review Amos 5:18–27. What were the three descriptions of the day of the Lord that Amos gave the people (5:18–20)? How did these pictures not line up with what the people were expecting Amos to say? How did these descriptions reshape the people's understanding of the day of the Lord?

From the Commentary

> Amos looked back (Amos 5:25–27) and reminded the people of their relationship to Jehovah after He had delivered them from Egypt. God asked the Jews to give Him faith, obedience, and love; but at Mount Sinai, after vowing to serve God, the people worshipped a golden calf! (See Ex. 32.) Their forefathers sinned further by offering sacrifices to false gods even while Jehovah was leading the nation through the wilderness! (Stephen quotes this in Acts 7:42–43.)
>
> After the Jews settled in the Promised Land, two generations of leaders guided them in the way of the Lord. But by the time the third generation came along, the people had turned to the idols of the nations around them (Judg. 2:10–15). God chastened them by allowing these nations to enslave Israel in their own land. But the message Amos had for the people was that they would have to leave their land and go into exile wherever the Assyrians sent them. It meant the end of the northern kingdom (2 Kings 17:6ff.).
>
> —*Be Concerned*, pages 67–68

7. Why was it important for Amos to remind the people of their past? How might this have been received by the people who were awaiting a different kind of day of the Lord than Amos was describing? In what ways were the Israelites being ignorant? In what ways were they worse than ignorant?

From the Commentary

> The "woe" described in Amos 6:1–2 was addressed to both Judah ("Zion") and Israel ("Samaria") because both kingdoms were indifferent toward God's Word and the judgment that hung over them. They called themselves "the foremost nation" (v. 1 NIV) and enjoyed an unwarranted false confidence for several reasons.
>
> The first cause of their complacency was their geography. Situated on Mount Zion, Jerusalem was considered impregnable (Ps. 78:68–69; 132:13–18); and Samaria also had a seemingly secure position. But when God decided to deal with these cities, nothing could stop the enemy.
>
> As for their prosperity, government, and military strength, Amos had already exposed the folly of depending on them; for the heart of each nation was corrupt to the core.
>
> —*Be Concerned*, page 68

8. The notable men in Israel's government gave their opinion that the nation was safe and secure. Why did the people believe them over God's word? In what ways can confidence that's based on expert advice, statistics, and material resources miss the truth of the spiritual dimension of life? What is the inevitable result if God's people trust worldly "experts" at the expense of missing relevant spiritual truth?

More to Consider: Complacency is an insidious sin because it is based on lies, is motivated by pride, and leads to trusting something other than God (Zeph. 1:12). What persuades complacent people to consider themselves wealthy and totally self-reliant (Rev. 3:17)? How have complacent people actually lost everything that's important in the spiritual life? How does God often deal with complacent people?

From the Commentary

"It can't happen here!" was the motto of the complacent leaders. "If a day of judgment is coming, it's surely a long way off." Whenever anybody mentioned the possibility of national disaster, the leaders laughed at the idea and disregarded it. But God had a different viewpoint. He said, "All the sinners of My people shall die by the sword, who say, 'The calamity shall not overtake nor confront us'" (Amos 9:10 NKJV). Yet by their very indifference, they were bringing the day of judgment that much nearer.

Amos described their indulgent way of life—a way of life that left no place for the disciplines of the spiritual life. They were living for pleasure, not for the glory of God. The common people usually slept on mats placed on the ground, but the wealthy enjoyed the luxury of beds of ivory and luxurious couches. They also used ivory to decorate their mansions (3:15). Excavations in Samaria have led to the discovery of the "Samaritan Ivories," fragments of beautiful ivory carvings that once adorned their houses and furniture.

The wealthy also enjoyed elegant feasts, eating lamb and veal, drinking wine in abundance, enjoying beautiful music, and wearing expensive perfumes. The poor people, whom they exploited, couldn't afford to kill tender lambs and calves, but had to settle for occasional mutton and beef, perhaps from a sacrifice. They would serve only cups of wine, not bowls; and their only "cosmetic" was olive oil.

—*Be Concerned*, pages 69–70

9. Review Amos 6:3–7. Is there anything inherently wrong with enjoying good food or music? Explain. What is the core of Amos's warning in this passage? Why does wealth so quickly become a deterrent to faith? What is the antidote to that disease?

From the Commentary

"I abhor the pride of Jacob, and hate his palaces; therefore I will deliver up the city and all that is in it" (Amos 6:8 NKJV). The Lord not only said this, but He also swore by Himself to fulfill it, which makes it a most solemn statement. The phrase "pride of Jacob" (KJV says "excellency of Jacob") is used in Psalm 47:4 to mean "the Promised Land." God abhorred the very land of Israel, the land He had given to His people for their inheritance.

Jesus said, "That which is highly esteemed among men is abomination in the sight of God" (Luke 16:15). The people boasted of their fortresses, their mansions, and their elegant way of life, all of which God abhorred and would one day destroy. We're reminded of the destruction of the great Babylonian world system described in Revelation 17—18. People who live without God, whose god is really personal pleasure, will one day hear Him say, "Fool! This night your soul will be required of you; then whose will those things be which you have provided?" (Luke 12:20 NKJV).

—Be Concerned, pages 71–72

10. Review Amos 6:8–14. This passage is about those who are impudent toward God. What does it mean to be impudent? What were the judgments Amos listed that these people would face? This is the last part of Amos's message to the complacent kingdom of Israel. Why did he end with such a strong message of judgment? How did this set the table for the message about God's coming kingdom that followed?

Looking Inward

Take a moment to reflect on all that you've explored thus far in this study of Amos 5—6. Review your notes and answers and think about how each of these things matters in your life today.

Tips for Small Groups: To get the most out of this section, form pairs or trios and have group members take turns answering these questions. Be honest and as open as you can in this discussion, but most of all, be encouraging and supportive of others. Be sensitive to those who are going through particularly difficult times and don't press for people to speak if they're uncomfortable doing so.

11. What are the different ways you actively seek the Lord? What happens to your witness when you do that diligently? What happens to your witness when you stop seeking?

12. Have you ever felt ashamed to stand up against something that was wrong? Explain. How can you find the strength to speak boldly about God's truth?

13. Describe a time when you were tempted to pursue "the good life" even though it could have had a negative impact on your faith life. What is it about possessions that tempts you? If you're wealthy (and in the world's perspective, it's most likely true that you are), how do you keep a healthy attitude toward that wealth?

Going Forward

14. Think of one or two things that you have learned that you'd like to work on in the coming week. Remember that this is all about quality, not quantity. It's better to work on one specific area of life and do it well than to work on many and do poorly (or to be so overwhelmed that you simply don't try).

Do you want to take action to avoid becoming complacent in your faith? Be specific. Go back through Amos 5—6 and put a star next to the phrase or verse that is most encouraging to you. Consider memorizing this verse.

Real-Life Application Ideas: This week, make a plan to seek the Lord diligently in as many ways as possible. Start with a focused time of Bible reading, but don't stop there. Set aside time for prayer and use that time to listen for God's voice. Talk with close friends or family members about what God is revealing to them in their lives. Listen for clues about how God is speaking to others in order to better hear His voice in your own life. Attend worship with an open heart, waiting on God to reveal Himself to you. And don't forget to be aware of God's role in the everyday of work and family life too. Seeking God takes intentional effort—but the reward is well worth it.

Seeking Help

15. Write a prayer below (or simply pray one in silence), inviting God to work on your mind and heart in those areas you've noted in the Going Forward section. Be honest about your desires and fears.

Notes for Small Groups:

- *Look for ways to put into practice the things you wrote in the Going Forward section. Talk with other group members about your ideas and commit to being accountable to one another.*

- *During the coming week, ask the Holy Spirit to continue to reveal truth to you from what you've read and studied.*

- *Before you start the next lesson, read Amos 7—9. For more in-depth lesson preparation, read chapter 6, "Stop—Look—Listen!," in* Be Concerned.

Listen!
(AMOS 7—9)

Before you begin ...
- *Pray for the Holy Spirit to reveal truth and wisdom as you go through this lesson.*
- *Read Amos 7—9. This lesson references chapter 6 in* Be Concerned. *It will be helpful for you to have your Bible and a copy of the commentary available as you work through this lesson.*

Getting Started

From the Commentary

The prophecy of Amos concludes with the record of five special visions of judgment that God gave to His servant: the locusts (7:1–3), the fire (vv. 4–6), the plumb line (vv. 7–9), the basket of fruit (8:1–14), and the ruined temple (9:1–10). However, the prophet closes his message on a positive note as he describes the future glorious kingdom that God has promised to His people (vv. 11–15).

—*Be Concerned*, page 77

1. How might the Israelites have received the five judgments that came at the end of Amos's prophecy? God seemed to speak a message of doom and gloom often to His wayward people. What did this say about God's expectations of His people? How did God offer hope in the final piece of Amos's message?

2. Choose one verse or phrase from Amos 7—9 that stands out to you. This could be something you're intrigued by, something that makes you uncomfortable, something that puzzles you, something that resonates with you, or just something you want to examine further. Write that here.

Going Deeper

From the Commentary

> The life of a prophet wasn't easy. On the one hand, he had to stay close to the Lord in order to hear His words and be able to share them with the people. But on the other hand, he also had to be with the people to whom he was ministering, and they didn't always want to accept his ministry. It's no wonder that some of the prophets wanted to resign, including Moses and Jeremiah. Amos had two

struggles: one with the Lord and one with the authorities, especially the king and his priest.

—*Be Concerned*, pages 77–78

3. Review Amos 7. What were Amos's struggles with the Lord (vv. 1–9)? What were his struggles with the authorities (vv. 10–17)? How were these similar to the struggles the disciples faced in the New Testament? How are they similar to the struggles believers face today?

From the Commentary

Amos was a true patriot who loved God and loved his nation, and it grieved him that he had to tell Israel and Judah that judgment was coming (Amos 7:1–9). No doubt there were times when he wished he was back at Tekoa caring for the sycamore trees and the sheep. But the Sovereign Lord ("Lord GOD," used eleven times in these three chapters) was in control of history, and Amos knew that God's will was best. The prophet saw three visions of judgment and responded to them.

First, Amos saw the vision of the locusts (vv. 1–3) as they were poised to attack the second crop late in the summer, after the king had taken his share (1 Kings 4:7). This was the farmers' last chance for a harvest, and the harvest would be destroyed. The summer heat was on its way, and there would be no more chance for a crop. Being a man of the soil himself, Amos would sympathize with these farmers.

—*Be Concerned*, page 78

4. Does it surprise you that it was God who prepared the insects and told them what to do? In what ways does it seem that God turned against His own people? How did Amos's prayer change God's plan? Consider other intercessors in the Bible, including Abraham (Gen. 18), Moses (Ex. 32; Num. 14), Samuel (1 Sam. 12), Elijah (1 Kings 18), and Paul (Rom. 9:1–3; 10:1–2). Do you think this kind of intercession is for the rare person with a special role, or is it for many Christians? Why?

More to Consider: Amos argued that the nation was so small it could never survive the plague of locusts. Why didn't Amos plead any of the covenant promises of God? (See Deut. 28:38–42.) Why did God heed the prophet's plea and relent in this story but not in others?

From Today's World

Today's church is as fractured as it ever was, divided and defined by differences of interpretation and opinion on matters of theology and practice and even culture. Some churches are notable for their strict adherence to a traditional interpretation of Scripture, while others forge their places in the world by embracing the most significant biblical truths in light of a changing, dynamic culture. But in all cases, churches continue to pursue the same big idea: understanding what it means to love God and love others. And while some churches purport to have direct lines to God as in the days of the prophets, most listen with eager ears to a God who seems to be speaking in a quieter voice than He once did.

5. Why do today's churches often struggle to "hear" God? Why might God have chosen to speak in a different way than He once did? What are some of the ways today's leaders might wish they could sway God's actions, as Amos did when he interceded on behalf of the Israelites?

From the Commentary

The third vision was that of the plumb line (Amos 7:7–9), an instrument used to test whether a wall was straight and true. A man stood on top of the wall and dropped a line with a weight on it. By matching the line to the wall, the workers could tell if the wall was upright.

God's law is His plumb line, and He measures His people to see how true they are to the pattern in His Word, and if they are of upright character and conduct. "Also I will make justice the measuring line, and righteousness the plummet" (Isa. 28:17 NKJV). Alas, in Amos's time, He

found that Israel was "out of plumb" and therefore had
to be destroyed. This would include Israel's high places
and sanctuaries, where they worshipped contrary to
God's law, for the only place the Jews were to bring their
sacrifices was to the temple in Jerusalem (Lev. 17:1–7).

—*Be Concerned*, page 79

6. Review Amos 7:7–9. "I will spare them no longer" is an ominous
statement. How had the nation of Israel gone too far? Why did the nation
of Israel seem to reach this place of hopelessness so often in their history?
How did God answer this apparent hopelessness?

From the Commentary

Amos proclaimed the word of the Lord to Amaziah and
informed him of the judgment that God would send on
him and his family. Amaziah would lose all his prop-
erty, go into exile, and die far from his native land. The
Assyrian soldiers would slay his sons. His wife would be
left destitute and would become a prostitute. The nation
of Israel would go into exile and be no more. It would be
quite a change from serving as the king's chief religious
leader at Bethel!

—*Be Concerned*, page 81

7. Review Amos 7:10–17. Describe the difference between Amaziah's and Amos's sources of power and influence. Why does God often call on humble servants to speak out against people of influence and authority in the world? What does this teach us about humility? About how God speaks His truth to the world? About how God can use us?

From the Commentary

After his painful encounter with Amaziah, Amos received further messages from the Lord; for it's just like the Master to encourage His servants after they've been through tough times (see Acts 18:9–11; 27:21–26; 2 Tim. 4:16–17).

God often used common objects to teach important spiritual truths, objects like pottery (Jer. 18—19), seed (Luke 8:11), yeast (Matt. 16:6, 11), and in Amos 8:1–3, a basket of summer (ripe) fruit. Just as this fruit was ripe for eating, the nation of Israel was ripe for judgment. The Hebrew word translated "summer" or "ripe" in verse 1 (*qayis*) is similar to the word translated "end" in verse 2 (*qes*). It was the end of the harvest for the farmers, and it would be the end for Israel when the harvest judgment came (see Jer. 1:11–12 for a similar lesson). "The harvest is past, the summer is ended, and we are not saved" (Jer. 8:20).

There comes a time when God's longsuffering runs out
(Isa. 55:6–7) and judgment is decreed. The songs at the
temple would become funeral dirges with weeping and
wailing, and corpses would be thrown everywhere and
not given proper burial. It would be a bitter harvest for
Israel as the nation reaped what it sowed. People would be
so overwhelmed that they would be unable to discuss the
tragedy. Silence would reign in the land.

—*Be Concerned*, pages 81–82

8. Review Amos 8:1–6. Why did God's longsuffering eventually run
out? How might this have been part of His overall plan? Why did Amos
declare that the end was coming? How had God's people rebelled against
the commandments concerning their relationship with God and their
relationship with others?

*More to Consider: One of the most egregious of sins the people
committed was trampling on the poor and needy and robbing them
of the little they possessed (Amos 8:4). How did Amos respond to this?
(See 2:6–7; 4:1; 5:11–12.) How is this an issue worthy of discussion in
today's church? Is lack of action in reaching out to the poor and needy
as sinful as these direct actions by the Israelites? Why or why not?
What is a godly response today to those who suffer in poverty?*

From the Commentary

The prophet used four pictures to describe the terror of the coming judgment. The first was that of an earthquake (Amos 8:8) with the land heaving like the rising waters of the Nile River. (The Nile rose about twenty-five feet during its annual flooding stage.) Even the land would shudder because of the people's sins. Earlier, Amos referred to an earthquake (1:1), but we aren't sure whether it was the fulfillment of this prophecy.

God would also visit them with darkness (Amos 8:9), perhaps an eclipse. (There was one in 763 BC.) The day of the Lord will be a day of darkness (Isa. 13:9–10; Joel 2:30–31).

The third picture is that of a funeral (Amos 8:10), with all their joyful feasts turned into mourning and wailing. Instead of being dressed elegantly and going to banquets or concerts, the people would wear sackcloth and join in mourning. Parents mourned greatly if an only son died, because that meant the end of the family name and line. But God's judgment would mean the end of a nation.

Finally, the judgment would be like a famine (vv. 11–14), not only of literal food but also of spiritual nourishment. "Man shall not live by bread alone, but by every word that proceeds from the mouth of God" (Matt. 4:4 NKJV; see Deut. 8:3). In times of crisis, people turn to the Lord for some word of guidance or encouragement; but for Israel, no word would come. "We are given no miraculous signs;

no prophets are left, and none of us knows how long this will be" (Ps. 74:9 NIV).

—Be Concerned, page 83

9. Why would God call on such dramatic actions in response to His people's sins? How do you think the people received this threat of destruction? How would the threat of famine—both food and spiritual nutrition— have affected the people? God had proved Himself to be truthful in the past, so why would His people even doubt His judgment at this point? And yet many did. Does the modern church sometimes blindly disregard God's truth like this? If so, how?

From the Commentary

In the final chapter of the book, the prophet Amos shares four affirmations from the heart of the Lord— three of which deal with judgment and the fourth with mercy.

(1) "I will strike!" (Amos 9:1). In a vision, Amos saw the Lord standing by an altar and announcing that the worshippers would be slain because the building would be destroyed and fall upon them. This was probably not the temple in Jerusalem because Amos was sent to the northern kingdom of Israel; and when the Babylonians destroyed the temple in Jerusalem, it was by fire (Jer. 52:12–13). This may have been the king's royal chapel in Bethel, although we don't know what kind of building that was. God's warning in Amos 3:13–15 seems to parallel this vision, describing what the Assyrian army would do when it entered the land.

The altar was the place of sacrifice and the atonement, but God refused to accept their sacrifices and forgive their sins (5:21–23). Their man-made religion, carried on by unauthorized priests, was an abomination to the Lord; and He would now destroy it.

(2) "I will search!" (Amos 9:2–4). Any idolatrous worshipper who tried to escape would be tracked down and slain. Though they run down into sheol, the realm of the dead, God would search them out; and if they could reach heaven, there would be no protection there. They couldn't hide from God on the highest mountain or in the depths of the sea (see Ps. 139:7–12). Even if they were taken captive to a foreign land, He would find them and judge them. His eye would be upon them for judgment, not for blessing (33:18; 34:15; Rev. 6:12–17).

(3) "I will destroy!" (Amos 9:5–10). Nine times in the book, Amos calls God "the Lord of hosts," that is, "the Lord of the armies of heaven and earth." … The people of Israel created their gods in their own image and held such a low view of Jehovah that they thought He would approve of their sinful ways.

Amos reminded them of the greatness of the God they thought they were worshipping. He is the God of creation, who can melt the earth with a touch and make the land rise and fall like the swelling of the Nile River. He controls the heavens, the earth, and the seas, and no one can stay His hand.

But He is always the God of mercy (vv. 8–10), who will keep His covenant with Abraham and his descendants and not destroy the nation. The nations would be sifted, and the sinners punished, but not one of His true worshippers would be lost. It's always the believing remnant that God watches over so that they might fulfill His will on the earth. The self-confident sinners, who don't expect to be punished, are the ones who will be slain by the sword (v. 10).

(4) "I will restore!" (Amos 9:11–15). In contrast to God's destroying the Israelite house of false worship, God will raise up the "hut" of David, thereby assuring a bright future for the people of Israel and Judah. Like a rickety shack, David's dynasty was about to collapse. From the Babylonian captivity to this present hour, there has been no Davidic king ruling over the Jews; and though a Jewish nation has been restored, they have no king, priest, temple, or sacrifice.

—Be Concerned, pages 84–86

10. How does the end of Amos's book speak to hope for the future? What did Amos reveal about God's heart in this closing chapter? What did he reveal about God's love?

Looking Inward

Take a moment to reflect on all that you've explored thus far in this study of Amos 7—9. Review your notes and answers and think about how each of these things matters in your life today.

> *Tips for Small Groups: To get the most out of this section, form pairs or trios and have group members take turns answering these questions. Be honest and as open as you can in this discussion, but most of all, be encouraging and supportive of others. Be sensitive to those who are going through particularly difficult times and don't press for people to speak if they're uncomfortable doing so.*

11. Have you ever felt as if God had turned against you? Describe that time. What made it seem that way? How did God use that circumstance to change you? How did you grow from that experience?

12. If you could sway God's actions in the world, what would you ask Him to do? What does this reveal about your heart toward God? Toward people? Instead of asking God to "change His mind," what are other ways to seek the answers to your biggest faith questions?

13. Have you ever felt humbled by something God asked you to do? Describe that experience. How did God reveal His intent? How did you respond? How easy or difficult is it to trust God's hand when He's asking you to do a difficult thing? Why?

Going Forward

14. Think of one or two things that you have learned that you'd like to work on in the coming week. Remember that this is all about quality, not quantity. It's better to work on one specific area of life and do it well than

to work on many and do poorly (or to be so overwhelmed that you simply don't try).

Do you want to be an intercessor between people and God? Be specific. Go back through Amos 7—9 and put a star next to the phrase or verse that is most encouraging to you. Consider memorizing this verse.

Real-Life Application Ideas: Much of Amos's message is about all that the people were doing wrong. But the final chapter shows a thread of hope, a reminder to the people that God is true to His promises—and those promises include a bright future for His people. This week, take a break from focusing on all that's going wrong in the world in general, and in your life in specific. Instead, let this be a time of holding on to hope for the future, whether that hoped-for future happens during this life or the next. Listen for God's promises in everyday activities—at work, at home, at church. Wherever you happen to be, seek the hope that God promises through Jesus. You can go back to contemplating the harder stuff next week, but with a renewed sense of grace.

Seeking Help

15. Write a prayer below (or simply pray one in silence), inviting God to work on your mind and heart in those areas you've noted in the Going Forward section. Be honest about your desires and fears.

Notes for Small Groups:
- *Look for ways to put into practice the things you wrote in the Going Forward section. Talk with other group members about your ideas and commit to being accountable to one another.*
- *During the coming week, ask the Holy Spirit to continue to reveal truth to you from what you've read and studied.*
- *Before you start the next lesson, read the book of Obadiah. For more in-depth lesson preparation, read chapter 7, "A Tale of Two Brothers," in* Be Concerned.

Two Brothers
(OBADIAH)

Before you begin …
- *Pray for the Holy Spirit to reveal truth and wisdom as you go through this lesson.*
- *Read the book of Obadiah. This lesson references chapter 7 in* Be Concerned. *It will be helpful for you to have your Bible and a copy of the commentary available as you work through this lesson.*

Getting Started

From the Commentary

We know very little about the prophet Obadiah except that he wrote the prophecy bearing his name (the shortest book in the Old Testament) and that his name means "one who worships God." At least twelve other men in Scripture had this name, four of whom were connected in some way with the ministry at the temple (1 Chron. 9:16; 2 Chron. 34:12; Neh. 10:5; 12:25).

Students aren't even agreed as to when the events occurred that are described in Obadiah 10–14. The traditional view is that Obadiah was referring to the Babylonian invasion of Judah and the destruction of Jerusalem in 586 BC. The psalmist states that the Edomites encouraged the Babylonians as the army razed the city (Ps. 137:7), but there is no evidence that the Edomites actually entered Jerusalem at that time or tried to stop the Jews from escaping.

Some Old Testament scholars think that Obadiah's reference is to an earlier invasion of Jerusalem by the Philistines and Arabians, at which time Edom assisted the invaders and broke free from Judah's control (2 Chron. 21:8–10, 16–17). This would have been during the reign of weak King Jehoram (853–841 BC), who married King Ahab's daughter and led Judah into sin. God permitted the invasion of the land and the plundering of Jerusalem as a punishment for the king's disobedience.

—*Be Concerned*, page 89

1. Does it matter which invasion Obadiah is referencing in his prophecy? Why or why not? How can God use the truth in this book despite our lack of clarity on what historical events Obadiah was referencing?

2. Choose one verse or phrase from the book of Obadiah that stands out to you. This could be something you're intrigued by, something that makes you uncomfortable, something that puzzles you, something that resonates with you, or just something you want to examine further. Write that here.

Going Deeper

From the Commentary

Of all human conflicts, the most painful and difficult to resolve are those between blood relatives. But if family feuds are tragic, national feuds are even worse. Almost every nation has experienced a civil war, with brother killing brother in order to perpetuate a long-standing disagreement that nobody fully understands or wants to settle. History records that the roots of these disputes are bitter, long, and deep, and that every attempt to pull them up and destroy them usually meets with failure.

Esau and Jacob were twin brothers who had been competitors from before birth (Gen. 25:19–26). Unfortunately, their parents disagreed over the boys, with Isaac partial to Esau and Rebekah favoring Jacob. God had chosen Jacob, the younger son, to receive the blessing attached to the Abrahamic covenant (Rom. 9:10–12), but Jacob and Rebekah decided to get this blessing by scheming instead of trusting God (Gen. 27).

When Esau learned that his clever brother had stolen the blessing, he resolved to kill him after their father was dead, and this led to Jacob's leaving home to find a wife among his mother's relatives (vv. 41–46). Years later, the two brothers experienced a brief time of reconciliation (chap. 32), and they both faithfully attended the burial of Isaac (35:27–29), but the animosity was never removed. Esau established the nation of Edom (25:30; 35:1; 36:1ff.), and his descendants carried on the family feud that Esau had begun years before.

The law of Moses commanded the Jews to treat the Edomites like brothers: "You shall not abhor an Edomite, for he is your brother" (Deut. 23:7 NKJV). In spite of this, the Edomites "harbored an ancient hostility" against Israel (Ezek. 35:5 NIV) and used every opportunity to display it.

—*Be Concerned*, pages 91–92

3. Why is this background information important for our understanding of the book of Obadiah? Why was the message of brotherhood important to the divided people? How is it equally important for our world today in which the church is so divided?

From the Commentary

Like Isaiah (1:1), Micah (1:1), Nahum (1:1), and Habakkuk (1:1), the prophet Obadiah received his message from the Lord by means of a vision. "Surely the Lord GOD does nothing unless He reveals His secret counsel to His servants the prophets" (Amos 3:7 NASB). Obadiah wrote the vision so it could be shared with others and eventually become a part of the Holy Scriptures.

The Lord enabled Obadiah to know what was going on among the nations that were allied with Edom against Judah. Thanks to today's international media coverage and the instant transmission of information, very little can happen in political and diplomatic arenas without the world knowing about it. But in Obadiah's day, the travels of national leaders and their political discussions were secret. There were no newspapers or press conferences.

God told His servant that an ambassador from a nation allied with Edom was visiting the other nations to convince their leader to join forces and attack Edom. Actually, it was the Lord who had ordained this change in policy, and what appeared to be just another diplomatic visit was actually the working out of the Lord's judgments against Edom. This was the beginning of the fulfillment of the prophecy in Obadiah 7, "All your allies will force you to the border" (NIV).

—*Be Concerned*, pages 92–93

4. Why does God so often speak to His prophets by way of vision? How does this provide a challenge for the prophets? John Wesley is said to have read the newspaper to see how God was governing His world, and this is certainly a biblical approach. In what ways did God rule over kingdoms and nations in biblical times (2 Chron. 20:6; Dan. 5:21)? How is this similar to how God rules our nations today? Does this mean that God is to blame for any foolish or wicked decisions and deeds of government officials? Explain.

From the History Books

Throughout history, the church has enjoyed seasons of renewal and revival. Many of those came with great proclamations of Jesus' "soon arrival." Self-proclaimed prophets would hang their ministries on the very idea that the "signs and wonders" were pointing clearly to Jesus' second coming. This often resulted in lots of people coming to Christ, perhaps as much out of fear of being left behind as being convinced about the need for redemption. But then time would go on and Jesus still hadn't returned. In recent times, there haven't been as many claims of Jesus' "soon return," but that doesn't mean churches still don't look to the sky with eagerness and hopefulness.

5. What is it about the promise—or threat—of Jesus' return that draws people to a life of faith? Does the path someone takes to faith ultimately

matter? How can fear be used to motivate people to consider God's truth? When is it wrong to use fear tactics to stir people to consider a life of faith?

From the Commentary

In Obadiah 2–9, the prophet declared that God would judge Edom and take away everything the nation boasted about and depended on for security.

What kind of judgment did God promise to send to the nation of Edom? To begin with, He said *He would bring down their pride* (vv. 2–4). Edom was a proud nation that considered itself impregnable and invulnerable because it was situated "in the clefts of the rock" (v. 3), a region of rugged mountains with high cliffs and narrow valleys that would dissuade any invader from attacking. Like the eagles, the Edomites lived on the rocks and looked down from the heights with disdain upon the nations around them. The Edomites thought they were a great people, but God said He would make them small, which means "paltry." "Pride goes before destruction, a haughty spirit before a fall" (Prov. 16:18 NIV).

—*Be Concerned*, pages 93–94

6. Pride is a common theme in the New and Old Testaments. Why is it such an egregious sin? Review Obadiah 5–6. How would "plundering the Edomites' wealth" have affected the Edomites' pride? Why must pride be removed before a people can come close to God?

From the Commentary

> Though protected by their lofty heights, the Edomites were smart enough to know that they needed friends to help them stand against the great empires that frequently threatened the smaller Eastern nations. Edom would also want allies to assist them in their constant feud with Israel (see Ps. 83:5–8). But God would turn these friends into enemies, and those who had eaten with them and made covenants of peace would break those covenants. While pretending to be friends, their allies would turn into traitors, set a trap, and catch Edom by surprise.
>
> —*Be Concerned*, pages 94–95

7. Why is boasting so dangerous for a nation? How can pride turn a nation to ruin? How is this evident in today's political climate?

From the Commentary

> Having announced what God was going to do to Edom, Obadiah then proceeded to defend God's judgment of the nation (Obad. 10–16). The Edomites were guilty of at least four abominable sins, the first of which was using violence against their brothers, the Jews (vv. 10–11). When their founder, Esau, discovered he was deprived of his father's blessing, he determined to kill his brother, Jacob (Gen. 27:41), and this malicious attitude was passed along to his descendants. If you had asked them, "Are you your brother's keeper?" they would have replied, "No! We're our brother's killer!"
>
> Instead of assisting their brothers in their plight, the Edomites stood "on the other side" (see Luke 10:30–32) and watched the enemy soldiers cast lots for the spoils, including the captive Jews, who would become slaves. The Edomites acted like the enemy instead of behaving like blood brothers of the Jews.
>
> A word from Solomon is appropriate here: "Deliver those who are drawn toward death, and hold back those stumbling to the slaughter. If you say, 'Surely we did not know this,' does not He who weighs the hearts consider it? He who keeps your soul, does He not know it?" (Prov. 24:11–12 NKJV). Also, a word from the prophet Amos: "For three sins of Edom, even for four, I will not turn back my wrath. Because he pursued his brother with a sword, stifling all compassion, because his anger raged continually and his fury flamed unchecked" (Amos 1:11 NIV).

Not only did the Edomites ignore the plight of the Jews, but also *they rejoiced at what the enemy was doing* (Obad. 12; see Ezek. 35:15; 36:5). For the Jews, this was a day of destruction and distress; but for the Edomites, it was a day of delight and rejoicing. In their pride, Edom looked down on the Jews and gloated over their misfortune.

—*Be Concerned*, pages 95–96

8. What causes someone to cheer on the suffering of others? Is this always wrong? What would a godly response to the Jews' plight have been? Read Proverbs 24:17–18. How did this message apply to the Edomites? How does it apply to us today?

More to Consider: How did God respond after Pharaoh ordered all the Jewish baby boys drowned (Ex. 1; 14:26–31)? What happened to the men who lied about Daniel in order to have Daniel thrown to the lions (Dan. 6)? What does this say about God's judgments (Rev. 16:7)? How does this apply to the Edomites' story?

From the Commentary

Now that the prophecy about Edom has been delivered, Obadiah turns to his own people and announces three divine promises.

The first promise is God will deliver you (Obad. 17–18). God did deliver His people from Babylonian captivity, and He will again deliver them in the last days and establish His kingdom. Mount Zion will be consecrated to the Lord and all defilement removed. "Jacob" refers to the southern kingdom and "Joseph" the northern kingdom. They will be united into one nation and enter the messianic kingdom together, possessing the inheritance promised to them. It appears from Isaiah 11:10–16, a parallel passage, that Moab and Edom will be restored as nations in the last days, but the Jews will burn them as stubble. (See Ex. 15:7; Isa. 10:17; and Matt. 3:12 for parallels.)

The second promise is God will defeat your enemies (Obad. 19–20). Israel will reclaim the land formerly inhabited by the Edomites (the Negev), the Philistines (the Shephelah), and the Samaritans (Ephraim). The Jews have been struggling to possess their inheritance for centuries, but other powers have always stood in the way. The Jews will "possess their possessions" (v. 17) without the help of any nation, but only through the help of the Lord their God. Israel has returned to their land in unbelief, and the nation was established in 1948. However, one day they shall see their Messiah and believe on Him, and the nation will be "born in a day" (Isa. 66:8; Zech. 12:10—13:1; 14:1–9).

—*Be Concerned*, page 98

9. How would the promises mentioned in the previous commentary excerpt help encourage the embattled Israelites? Why is deliverance such a key theme in the Israelites' story? What parallels does this theme have in the New Testament story? How does this theme of inheritance continue to be significant in the story of the Jewish people?

From the Commentary

The third promise is God will establish the kingdom (Obad. 21). The Lord will reign from Mount Zion, where His temple will stand, "and all the nations will stream to it" (Isa. 2:2 NASB). It's interesting to note that King Messiah will have "deliverers" ("saviors" KJV) assist Him in His rule over the nations. This fact should be studied with reference to our Lord's promises to His apostles (Matt. 19:27–30) and those who are faithful to Him today (24:42–51; 25:14–30; Luke 19:11–27). Jesus teaches that faithfulness to Him today will mean reigning with Him in the kingdom.

—*Be Concerned*, pages 98–99

10. Read Revelation 11:15. How does this verse relate to the promise in Obadiah 21? What is our responsibility between now and the establishment of God's new kingdom?

Looking Inward

Take a moment to reflect on all that you've explored thus far in this study of the book of Obadiah. Review your notes and answers and think about how each of these things matters in your life today.

Tips for Small Groups: To get the most out of this section, form pairs or trios and have group members take turns answering these questions. Be honest and as open as you can in this discussion, but most of all, be encouraging and supportive of others. Be sensitive to those who are going through particularly difficult times and don't press for people to speak if they're uncomfortable doing so.

11. Describe a time when pride got in the way of accomplishing something for God. How did that circumstance affect your relationship with God? What does it take to humble you before God?

12. Have you ever felt the temptation to cheer when someone you didn't like was going through hard times? What is the source of that temptation? Why do you feel satisfaction when someone else is suffering? What is the biblical approach to those who suffer—even those whom you don't like or get along with?

13. Which of God's promises are you most excited about? How does the promise of a coming kingdom affect the way you live your life daily?

Going Forward

14. Think of one or two things that you have learned that you'd like to work on in the coming week. Remember that this is all about quality, not quantity. It's better to work on one specific area of life and do it well than to work on many and do poorly (or to be so overwhelmed that you simply don't try).

Do you want to repent of pride? Be specific. Go back through the book of Obadiah and put a star next to the phrase or verse that is most encouraging to you. Consider memorizing this verse.

Real-Life Application Ideas: The theme of two brothers in this book reminds us of the importance of working out differences whenever possible between family members. This week, consider any familial rifts in your own life, and with the wise counsel of a pastor or small-group leader and the guidance of the Holy Spirit through prayer, seek answers to repairing those rifts—or at the very least, find ways to forgive where forgiveness is required. Make this a week of healing.

Seeking Help

15. Write a prayer below (or simply pray one in silence), inviting God to work on your mind and heart in those areas you've noted in the Going Forward section. Be honest about your desires and fears.

Notes for Small Groups:
- *Look for ways to put into practice the things you wrote in the Going Forward section. Talk with other group members about your ideas and commit to being accountable to one another.*
- *During the coming week, ask the Holy Spirit to continue to reveal truth to you from what you've read and studied.*
- *Before you start the next lesson, read Micah 1—2. For more in-depth lesson preparation, read chapter 8, "Judgment Is Coming!," in* Be Concerned.

Judgment
(MICAH 1—2)

Before you begin …
- *Pray for the Holy Spirit to reveal truth and wisdom as you go through this lesson.*
- *Read Micah 1—2. This lesson references chapter 8 in* Be Concerned. *It will be helpful for you to have your Bible and a copy of the commentary available as you work through this lesson.*

Getting Started

From the Commentary

Micah's name is an abbreviated form of "Micaiah" and means "Who is like Jehovah?" (see Mic. 7:18). He was from the village of Moresheth near Gath, about twenty-five miles southwest of Jerusalem; he prophesied during the last half of the eighth century BC, during the reigns of Jotham (750–735), Ahaz (735–715), and Hezekiah (715–686). He was a contemporary of Isaiah (1:1) in Judah and Amos and Hosea (1:1) in Israel.

During Jotham's reign, Assyria grew stronger. When Ahaz ascended the throne, both Syria and Israel tried to pressure him into joining a rebellion against Assyria (Isa. 7). Jeremiah 26:18 informs us that it was the ministry of Micah that encouraged the great reformation in Judah under the leadership of King Hezekiah (2 Kings 18—20).

Society in Judah was rapidly changing from rural to urban. In defiance of the law of Moses, wealthy investors were buying up small family farms and developing huge land holdings, which created serious problems for the poor.

—*Be Concerned*, page 103

1. What are some of the dangers of a society that's changing from rural to urban? How could that have affected the Jewish nation? Once again God used someone who had a "common" background to speak His truth to the people. How might wealthy investors have viewed Micah and his farming background? How should they have viewed him?

More to Consider: Micah saw the coming judgment of Israel under Assyria as well as the fall of Jerusalem and Judah under the Babylonians. He sought to call the Jews back to faithful worship of Jehovah and sincere obedience to His covenant. What was their response? Why did the people refuse to listen to God? How is the way God uses people from common walks of life to share His truth repeated throughout biblical history? Were the results in those instances similar to what Micah saw? Explain.

2. Choose one verse or phrase from Micah 1—2 that stands out to you. This could be something you're intrigued by, something that makes you uncomfortable, something that puzzles you, something that resonates with you, or just something you want to examine further. Write that here.

Going Deeper

From the Commentary

> King David had a great many talented men in his army, but the most valuable were perhaps the men of Issachar, who had "understanding of the times, to know what Israel ought to do" (1 Chron. 12:32). Because they understood the times, the men of Issachar abandoned the ill-fated

house of Saul and joined forces with David, God's chosen king. They saw which way God's hand was moving, and they obediently moved in that direction.

Micah of Moresheth was a man who had the same kind of discernment because God gave him insight into the changes taking place on the national and international scene. Micah received three messages from the Lord to deliver to the people in hopes they would abandon their idolatry and return to sincere faith in the Lord.

—*Be Concerned*, page 105

3. What were the main points of the messages God asked Micah to deliver to the people in Micah 1—2? How important was the character of a person God chose to prophesy? Why is discernment such a key component in the lives of those whom God calls? How do we see this character trait in Micah's life?

From the Commentary

When the prophet Amos was about to indict Israel and Judah, he started by condemning the Gentile nations around them (Amos 1—2); but the prophet Micah didn't take that approach. Without any formal introduction, he moved right into his message and sounded the alarm.

The image in Micah 1:2–5 is that of a court of law, with God as the Judge and Judah and Samaria as the defendants. Micah addresses all the people of the earth because God is the Lord of the whole earth (Mic. 4:2–3) and all the nations are accountable to Him. God is both Judge and Witness from His holy temple, where His law was kept in the ark of the covenant. A holy God must act in righteousness and judge sin.

Today when a judge enters a courtroom from his or her chamber, everybody in the courtroom rises—a symbol of the respect we have for the judge and the law that he or she represents. But no judge ever came to court in the manner described by Micah! The verb "to come forth" means "to come forth for battle." God opens the court and declares war!

A judge comes to court to see to it that justice is done, and he or she isn't allowed to take sides. But when God comes to judge the nations, He has all the evidence necessary and doesn't have to call any witnesses. God is angry at His people because of their sins. That's why His coming makes the earth split and the mountains melt so that the rock flows like melted wax or a waterfall.

—*Be Concerned*, page 106

4. Micah's approach to his message was different from Amos's. What's the point of diving right into the heart of the message? Why not a gentle introduction? How do you think the imagery of a court and judge affected the way the people received Micah's message?

From Today's World

The word *idolatry* sounds antiquated in today's church, yet idolatry persists in the modern church as much as, if not more so than, in the time of Micah and the other minor prophets. What once was represented by actual idols and pagan religions can now be defined in more worldly terms: *fame, fortune, money, power, success.* We may not have golden statues on the front lawns of our churches, but we do have plenty of things vying for our honor and love and loyalty that aren't the one true God. The church suffers from the same challenges today as God's people did millennia ago; only the names of the idols have changed.

5. In the simplest terms, what is idolatry? Why is idolatry such a persistent theme in the Old Testament books? What does idolatry look like in the New Testament? How does the modern church address this concern? Why is it so important to address idolatry in the modern church? What happens if we don't take it seriously?

From the Commentary

> The prophet responded to God's message by acting like a
> grieving man at a funeral (Mic. 1:6–8; 2 Sam. 15:30). He
> was genuinely burdened because of what would happen
> to his people if they didn't heed God's Word and turn
> from their sin.
>
> —*Be Concerned*, page 107

6. What did Micah's response to God's message (Mic. 1:8–9) reveal
about his heart? Why was he grieving? How did this kind of sincerity and
intensity affect the way others might have heard him? What implications
does this have for the manner in which leaders ought to lead today?

From the Commentary

> The capital city of the northern kingdom was situated on
> a hill that overlooked a fertile valley. The prophet Isaiah
> called the city "the crown of pride" with "glorious beauty"
> (Isa. 28:1) and predicted that God's judgment would
> destroy the city (vv. 2–4). The Assyrians would turn the

beautiful city into a heap of rubble, and her idols wouldn't be able to protect the city from its enemies.

The problem with Samaria was that she was toxic; her infection had spread to Judah. The prophet wept over his land the way you would weep over a patient with an incurable disease in the hospital (Mic. 1:9). Isaiah used a similar image to describe the plight of Judah (Isa. 1:5–6), and Jeremiah wept because the spiritual leaders in his day didn't deal drastically with the sin sickness of the people (Jer. 6:14; 7:8; 8:11).

Micah describes the ruin of the southern part of Judah (the Shephelah) by the invading Assyrians in 701 BC (Mic. 1:10–16; see 2 Kings 18:7ff.). They swept through the land and took forty-six cities, but they could not take Jerusalem because God protected it. Micah used a series of puns based on the names of the cities similar in sound to familiar Hebrew words. For example, "Gath" is similar to the Hebrew word for "tell." Thus he wrote, "Tell it not in Gath." Beth Ophrah means "house of dust." Thus he wrote, "Roll in the dust." The people of Shaphir ("pleasant, beautiful") would look neither beautiful nor pleasant as they were herded off as naked prisoners of war.

The roll call of cities goes on. The citizens of Zaanan ("come out") would not be able to come out because of the danger. Beth Ezel means "house of taking away," and the city would be taken away. Maroth is related to "mara/myrrh" and means "bitterness," and the city would experience bitter calamity ("writhe in pain" NIV).

—*Be Concerned*, pages 107–8

7. What was the purpose of using puns when describing the fates of the cities? What did this reveal about the power of words to the people of Micah's time? What does it say about the importance of words to God Himself? What does it teach us about the creativity of God?

From the Commentary

> How could the Lord Jehovah permit such suffering and shame to come to His covenant people? Were they not His special heritage? Was not the land His love gift to them? That was why He was punishing them! "You only have I chosen of all the families of the earth; therefore I will punish you for all your sins" (Amos 3:2 NIV). Privilege brings responsibility, and responsibility brings accountability. The prophet held them accountable for two particular sins.
>
> —*Be Concerned*, page 109

8. Review Micah 2:1–11. Describe the nature of the two sins Micah addressed in this passage. What did he mean by covetousness (vv. 1–5)?

Listening to false prophets (vv. 6–11)? What are the modern names for these sins?

More to Consider: It was God who spoke in Micah 2:7–13 as He defended His faithful servant. Why did Micah need defending? What were the leaders missing? What does the way we respond to God's Word reveal about our relationship to God? (See John 8:47.)

From the Commentary

Just as the false prophets attacked Jeremiah (5:31) and Amos (7:10–17) for preaching God's truth, so the false prophets attacked Micah for faithfully declaring the message of God. These men espoused a shallow theology that had no place for either sin or repentance. "We are God's special people," they argued, "and He would never permit these judgments to happen in the land." As long as the people participated in religious services, they would not incur the wrath of God, even if their hearts were not in their worship. The Jews were Abraham's children, and God would never break the promises He made to Abraham. Such were their false premises.

—*Be Concerned*, page 111

9. Review Micah 2:6–11. Why is a theology that doesn't have place for sin or repentance a shallow theology? What is a modern version of this kind of thinking? Why is a shallow theology so dangerous to faith?

From the Commentary

The faithful prophet must expose sin and announce judgment, but he must also provide consolation and hope for those who receive his message and turn to God. Consolation without true repentance is only giving false hope; it's saying "Peace, peace!" when there is no peace. But conviction without hope creates only hopelessness, like performing surgery without providing healing.

In Micah 2:12, the Lord seems to be speaking to the entire nation ("all of you, O Jacob … Israel" NIV), and His promise seems to reach ahead to the end times when Israel and Judah will be united and their King Messiah will reign over them. Micah describes a triumphant procession into the land, with King Messiah at the head and the Lord leading the people, just as He had led them out of Egypt (v. 13).

However, until that glorious day, God will deal with the "remnant" of His people. The "remnant" is a very important doctrine in the prophetic books, and there are many references to it. Though the nation of Israel might rebel against God, there would always be a faithful remnant that would trust Him and seek to do His will, and God would work because of the faith of this remnant.

—*Be Concerned*, pages 112–13

10. Respond to the following statement: Consolation without true repentance is only giving false hope. Why is this true for Micah and the other prophets? Why is it true today? What is the "remnant" truth in today's church? In what ways does the hope of our nation lie with the "remnant"?

Looking Inward

Take a moment to reflect on all that you've explored thus far in this study of Micah 1—2. Review your notes and answers and think about how each of these things matters in your life today.

Tips for Small Groups: To get the most out of this section, form pairs or trios and have group members take turns answering these questions. Be honest and as open as you can in this discussion, but most of all, be encouraging and supportive of others. Be sensitive to those who are going through particularly difficult times and don't press for people to speak if they're uncomfortable doing so.

11. Have you ever felt too "common" to be used by God in any significant way? Why did you feel this way? What does Micah's story (among many others) teach you about the kind of person God invites to speak His truth to others? In what ways are you like Micah?

12. What are some idols you are tempted to love more than God? What are you tempted to fear? Why do these things draw your attention away from God? How can you best address the temptation to follow other idols?

13. Covetousness was one of the key sins Micah addressed in his message from God. We could call this materialism today. What are some of the ways you deal with the temptation to have more possessions? Why is it easy to get trapped by that temptation? How does trusting God help you overcome that temptation?

Going Forward

14. Think of one or two things that you have learned that you'd like to work on in the coming week. Remember that this is all about quality, not quantity. It's better to work on one specific area of life and do it well than to work on many and do poorly (or to be so overwhelmed that you simply don't try).

Do you want to take a step away from being materialistic? Be specific. Go back through Micah 1—2 and put a star next to the phrase or verse that is most encouraging to you. Consider memorizing this verse.

Real-Life Application Ideas: The theme of this section of Micah is "return to God." Take some time this week to consider the places in your life where you've moved away from God. Perhaps you're leaving Him out of the workplace or forgetting to set aside family time with God. Be intentional in your efforts to grow closer to God in all areas of life. Then keep doing that. All relationships take work—and your relationship with God is the most important one you'll ever have. Don't make the same mistake the Israelites kept making over and over again.

Seeking Help

15. Write a prayer below (or simply pray one in silence), inviting God to work on your mind and heart in those areas you've noted in the Going Forward section. Be honest about your desires and fears.

Notes for Small Groups:

- *Look for ways to put into practice the things you wrote in the Going Forward section. Talk with other group members about your ideas and commit to being accountable to one another.*

- *During the coming week, ask the Holy Spirit to continue to reveal truth to you from what you've read and studied.*

- *Before you start the next lesson, read Micah 3—7. For more in-depth lesson preparation, read chapters 9 and 10, "A Ruler Is Coming!" and "'Thy Kingdom Come,'" in* Be Concerned.

The Kingdom
(MICAH 3—7)

Before you begin ...
- *Pray for the Holy Spirit to reveal truth and wisdom as you go through this lesson.*
- *Read Micah 3—7. This lesson references chapters 9 and 10 in* Be Concerned. *It will be helpful for you to have your Bible and a copy of the commentary available as you work through this lesson.*

Getting Started

From the Commentary

Micah's second message is at the heart of the book and focuses on Israel's future. Micah rebuked the leaders of the nation for their sinful conduct, which God would judge (3:1–12), and he outlined the events that would usher in the promised kingdom (4:1—5:15). Knowing that God has such a glorious future planned for their nation should have motivated the leaders to turn from their sins and obey the Lord. "Everyone who has this hope in him purifies himself, just as he is pure" (1 John 3:3 NIV).

—*Be Concerned*, page 117

1. How might the promise of a hoped-for future have changed the behavior of the Israelites? What was in fact their response to Micah's message? Why would they be motivated to change if they were enjoying their sinful choices?

More to Consider: As with Micah's other messages, this second message opens with a call for the people to "hear" what the Lord would say through His servant (1:2; 6:1). Read Hebrews 12:25. How is this similar to what Micah was saying? What are the dangers of turning a deaf ear to the voice of God when He speaks through His Word? (See Heb. 3:7–8.)

2. Choose one verse or phrase from Micah 3—7 that stands out to you. This could be something you're intrigued by, something that makes you uncomfortable, something that puzzles you, something that resonates with you, or just something you want to examine further. Write that here.

Going Deeper

From the Commentary

Micah fearlessly told the people their sins and warned them that judgment was coming, while the false prophets tickled the people's ears and told them what they wanted to hear.

Few men are as pitiable as those who claim to have a call from God yet tailor their sermons to please others. Their first rule is "Don't rock the boat"; their second is "Give people what they want." But a true servant of God declares God's message regardless of whether the people like it or not. He'd like to be a peacemaker, but sometimes he has to be a troublemaker. No wonder Jeremiah cried out, "Alas, my mother, that you gave me birth, a man with whom the whole land strives and contends!" (Jer. 15:10 NIV).

Micah also addressed *all the leaders of the land* (Mic. 3:9–12)—the rulers, the priests, and the prophets—and accused them of numerous sins: committing injustice, distorting the truth, murdering innocent people, accepting bribes, and while doing these evil deeds, claiming to be serving the Lord! "We are depending on the Lord," they said. "Is He not among us? Then nothing evil can happen to us." It was hypocrisy of the worst kind.

—*Be Concerned*, page 119

3. Review Micah 3:8. How does this describe the true prophet? What challenges did Micah face in dealing with the leaders of the land? How did their ignorance of the Lord's character and the terms of His covenant give them false confidence?

From the Commentary

Micah moved from the destruction of Jerusalem (606–586 BC) to "the last days," when there will be a new Jerusalem and a rebuilt temple at the heart of the righteous kingdom of Messiah. The period known as "the last days" began with the ministry of Christ (Heb. 1:1–2), and it climaxes with His return to establish His kingdom on earth. The Lord gave His people four wonderful promises.

(1) A promised kingdom (Mic. 4:1–8).

(2) A promised deliverance (Mic. 4:9–10).

(3) A promised conquest (Mic. 4:11–13).

(4) A promised King (Mic. 5:1–5a).

—*Be Concerned*, pages 120–22

4. Review each of the promises in Micah 4:1—5:5. In what ways did these promises provide an encouraging scenario for the people? Did the people appear to grasp the significance of these promises? What is a normal (and appropriate) response to promises such as these?

From the Commentary

> As he continued to view the distant scene, Micah announced that Israel's future enemies would be defeated (Mic. 5:5b–6), the Jewish remnant would be blessed (vv. 7–9), and the nation would be purged of its sins (vv. 10–15).
>
> "The Assyrian" named in verse 5 isn't the Assyrian army of Micah's day, for the Jews in that day certainly didn't defeat Assyria and rule over her land. The Assyrians soundly defeated Israel, and the land of Israel was ruined. "The Assyrian" is another way of saying "the enemy," and here it refers to Israel's enemies in the last days when all nations will gather against her (Zech. 10:10–11; 12:9; 14:1–3).
>
> Though small in number, the Jewish remnant of the last days will experience great help from the Lord as they face

their enemies. Micah used two similes to illustrate this blessing: the refreshing dew from heaven and the conquering strength of the lion. God will enable His people to overcome like lions and then bring fruitfulness to the world like the dew that watered Israel's crops (Ps. 133:3). Israel will triumph over her enemies through the power of the Lord.

In Micah's day, both Israel and Judah were guilty of sins that violated God's law and grieved God's heart. Time after time, He had sent messengers to the people to denounce their sins and warn of impending judgment, but the people wouldn't listen (2 Chron. 36:14–21). In the last days, Israel will return to her land in unbelief and practice these same sins. But God will purge the land and prepare them for a new life in the kingdom. They will see their Messiah, trust Him, and be saved (Zech. 12:10—13:1).

—*Be Concerned*, pages 124–25

5. Review Micah 5:5–15. What does this passage reveal about God's hope for His people? What are the various ways Christians today respond to promises about the coming kingdom? Why is it hard to trust a promised future, even with all the evidence in Scripture that God makes good on His promises?

From the Commentary

The prophet had delivered two of his three messages: a message of warning (Mic. 1—2) and a message of promise (chaps. 3—5). His third message was a challenge for the Jews to trust the Lord and obey His will, for only then could the nation escape terrible punishment and fulfill God's purposes in this world.

As you read Old Testament history and prophecy, keep in mind how important it was for Israel to be obedient to the Lord. God had raised up the nation to bring blessing to the whole world (Gen. 12:1–3), for it was through Israel that the Savior would come. "Salvation is of the Jews" (John 4:22). When the Jews began to adopt the practices of the godless nations around them, it defiled them and made them less able to do the work God had called them to do. It was because they despised their high and holy calling that the nation had to be chastened so severely.

—Be Concerned, page 129

6. Review Micah 6:1–8. Why did Micah present this third message in a courtroom-drama format? What arguments did he make to plead with his people to repent? How is this a message that can speak to the modern church?

From the Commentary

> The sins of the people were hidden behind a veneer of
> religious activity—routine worship that didn't come from
> their hearts. Micah's contemporary, the prophet Isaiah,
> told the people that the nation was sick from head to foot
> (Isa. 1:5–6) but wouldn't admit it, and that their "wor-
> ship" was nothing more than "trampling" the temple
> courts (v. 12). They were like the patient who asked the
> doctor to retouch his X-rays so he wouldn't have to endure
> surgery! His deceit didn't cure him; it made him worse.
>
> In this courtroom scene, the Lord called the witnesses
> (Mic. 6:1–2) and told the people to be prepared to plead
> their case.
>
> —*Be Concerned*, page 130

7. How did God open the proceedings of this court case? What did He
say about the way He had dealt with the nation from the very beginning?
What are some of the ways the Lord was longsuffering in His relationship
with the Israelites?

More to Consider: The phrase "from Shittim to Gilgal" (Mic. 6:5) reminded the people of Israel's crossing of the Jordan River and entering the Promised Land (Josh. 3—4). The same God who opened and closed the Red Sea also opened and closed the Jordan River so His people might claim their inheritance. He did for them what they couldn't do for themselves, but they didn't remember. Why is it important for God's people to learn from the past and remember it? (See these mentions of "remembering": Ex. 10:2; 13:8, 14; Deut. 6:20–25; Josh. 22:24; Ps. 78:1–8.)

From the Commentary

The people replied to God in Micah 6:6–7. But instead of confessing their sins or standing mute because their mouths had been shut by their sense of guilt (Rom. 3:19), they asked what they could do to get rid of their sins. Their request shows how shallow their spiritual life really was and that they were ignorant of the enormity of their sin and the high cost of forgiveness.

We get the impression that these questioners were interested in bargaining with God and "buying Him off," for they kept raising the bid. "Shall we bring a few calves as burnt offerings? If that's not enough, maybe we could offer a thousand sacrifices, such as Solomon offered [1 Kings 3:4; 8:63]? Would rivers of oil please Him? How about the ultimate sacrifice: our own flesh and blood offered on the altar, as Abraham did with Isaac?" But God doesn't bargain with sinners, and none of the sacrifices they offered to bring could have cleansed them from their sins.

—Be Concerned, page 131

8. Read Mark 10:17–27. How were the Israelites in Micah's time like the rich young man in this gospel account? How were they unlike the people at Pentecost who were cut to the heart and cried out, "What shall we do?" (Acts 2:37)? Why do people feel tempted to bargain with God in order to get "goodness" from Him?

From the Commentary

The prophet spoke to the people (Mic. 6:8) and told them exactly what the Lord wanted each of them to do. It was a personal matter that each individual sinner had to consider. His reply emphasized moral and ethical conduct, not religious ceremonies. Of course, we can't "do justly" unless we've been justified by faith and are right with God (Ps. 32:1–2; Rom. 4:1–8). And how can we "love mercy" if we've not personally experienced God's mercy (Eph. 2:4; Titus 3:5)? If we want to "walk humbly with [our]

God," we must first bow humbly before Him, confess our sins, and claim His promise of forgiveness (Luke 14:11; James 4:10).

Our Lord's parable about the Pharisee and publican in the temple (Luke 18:9–14) illustrates all three points. The publican was justified by faith, not by doing the kind of good works that the Pharisee boasted about. Since the publican depended on God's mercy to save him, he humbled himself before the Lord. The Pharisee, on the other hand, informed God (and whoever was listening in the temple) how good he was and therefore how much he deserved eternal life.

—*Be Concerned*, page 132

9. What is the main point of Micah 6:8? To whom is it directed? Is it wrong to make Micah 6:8 a message about salvation? Explain.

From the Commentary

The prophet reached a turning point when he looked away from the sins of the people and meditated on the faithfulness of the Lord. "But as for me, I watch in hope for the LORD, I wait for God my Savior; my God will hear me" (Mic. 7:7 NIV). He would "watch and pray" and put his trust only in the Lord. This verse is the "bridge" that connects the sections on sin and judgment with this closing section on hope.

In this final section of Micah's third message, we must distinguish several voices: the nation (vv. 8–10), the prophet (vv. 11–13), the Lord (vv. 14–15), and the prophet again (vv. 16–20). We must also realize that Micah is looking down through the centuries with prophetic vision to the time when Israel will come through the great tribulation to come, "dress rehearsals" as it were. But the future will bring victory to God's people, not defeat, when the Lord fulfills His promises and establishes the kingdom.

—*Be Concerned*, page 136

10. Review Micah 7:7–20. Why did Micah turn his focus to God's faithfulness? How might his audience have received that message after all the judgment messages? In what ways might the promise of a future victory, rather than an immediate one, have affected the way the people heard Micah's prophetic words?

Looking Inward

Take a moment to reflect on all that you've explored thus far in this study of Micah 3—7. Review your notes and answers and think about how each of these things matters in your life today.

Tips for Small Groups: To get the most out of this section, form pairs or trios and have group members take turns answering these questions. Be honest and as open as you can in this discussion, but most of all, be encouraging and supportive of others. Be sensitive to those who are going through particularly difficult times and don't press for people to speak if they're uncomfortable doing so.

11. What do you fear most about the future? How do God's promises help you face the uncertainty ahead of you? What frustrates you most about God's timing?

12. Have you ever attempted to bargain with God to get something you want? Describe one of those times. Why is it tempting to test God in this way? What does bargaining reveal about your level of trust in God? How can you change that?

13. What makes you impatient with God? What kinds of things do you wish He'd hurry up and fix? How can waiting patiently actually help you grow closer to Jesus? What does it take, practically speaking, to wait patiently on the Lord?

Going Forward

14. Think of one or two things that you have learned that you'd like to work on in the coming week. Remember that this is all about quality, not quantity. It's better to work on one specific area of life and do it well than to work on many and do poorly (or to be so overwhelmed that you simply don't try).

Do you want to be more patient while waiting on the Lord regarding some issue? Be specific. Go back through Micah 3—7 and put a star next

to the phrase or verse that is most encouraging to you. Consider memorizing this verse.

*Real-Life Application Ideas: Much of this section of Micah is dedicated
to the promise of God's coming kingdom—to a hopeful future where
all the ills and pains and challenges of the moment will be forgotten.
Take a moment to ponder some of those difficulties that you and your
loved ones are facing today. Then spend time each day this week
thanking God for His promises and asking Him to show you how to
live for Him when things are difficult. This week, focus on what it
means to trust God.*

Seeking Help

15. Write a prayer below (or simply pray one in silence), inviting God to
work on your mind and heart in those areas you've noted in the Going
Forward section. Be honest about your desires and fears.

Notes for Small Groups:

- *Look for ways to put into practice the things you wrote in the Going Forward section. Talk with other group members about your ideas and commit to being accountable to one another.*

- *During the coming week, ask the Holy Spirit to continue to reveal truth to you from what you've read and studied.*

- *Before you start the next lesson, read the book of Zephaniah. For more in-depth lesson preparation, read chapters 11 and 12, "There's a Great Day Coming!" and "The Glory of the Kingdom," in* Be Concerned.

Glory
(ZEPHANIAH)

Before you begin ...
- *Pray for the Holy Spirit to reveal truth and wisdom as you go through this lesson.*
- *Read Zephaniah. This lesson references chapters 11 and 12 in* Be Concerned. *It will be helpful for you to have your Bible and a copy of the commentary available as you work through this lesson.*

Getting Started

From the Commentary

Zephaniah's major theme is the day of the Lord, that period of time when God will judge the nations and usher in His righteous kingdom. This theme is found in almost all the prophets, but it is particularly evident in Joel and Zephaniah. "The great day of the LORD is near" (Zeph. 1:14 NIV).

The Scriptures reveal very little about Zephaniah's

personal life. He ministered in Judah during the time of King Josiah (640–609 BC), who led the nation in a religious reformation triggered by the finding of the book of the law in the temple in the year 622 (2 Chron. 34:14ff.). It's likely that Zephaniah preached prior to this reformation, or he would have said something about it in his book. Jeremiah and Zephaniah were contemporaries.

Politically, the times were in ferment. Assyria was losing its power, the Scythians were invading from the north, and Babylon had become the leading empire. King Manasseh (697–642 BC) had led the people of Judah deeper and deeper into idolatry and the adoption of foreign ideas and customs, and Josiah had sought to reverse this trend. Alas, King Josiah died on the battlefield before his work was finished, and his successors on the throne allowed the people to return to their sinful ways.

—*Be Concerned*, page 143

1. Why was the day of the Lord such a common theme for prophets? What exactly does it refer to? Why is it something to fear? In what ways is it something to look forward to?

2. Choose one verse or phrase from the book of Zephaniah that stands out to you. This could be something you're intrigued by, something that makes you uncomfortable, something that puzzles you, something that resonates with you, or just something you want to examine further. Write that here.

Going Deeper

From the Commentary

> You would expect the great-great-grandson of King Hezekiah to be living comfortably in Jerusalem, enjoying a life of ease. Instead, you find Zephaniah ministering as God's prophet, which was a dangerous calling. His contemporary, Jeremiah, was arrested and put in a filthy cistern for admonishing the leaders of Judah to surrender to the Babylonians.
>
> God had shown Zephaniah that judgment was coming upon Judah in the form of the Babylonian captivity, and the prophet had to share this message with the people. However, Babylon's invasion of Judah was but a feeble example of what would occur on that final day of the Lord, which would sweep over all the earth. Zephaniah

opened his book by presenting *three graphic pictures of the day of the Lord.*

The first picture is that of a *devastating universal flood* (Zeph. 1:2–3). The Hebrew word translated "consume" in the KJV means "to sweep away completely." The picture is that of total devastation of all that God created and is probably a reference to Noah's flood. (You find similar wording in Gen. 6:7; 7:4; 9:8–10.) God gave man dominion over the fish, the fowl, and the beasts (1:28; Ps. 8:7–8), but man lost that dominion when Adam disobeyed God. However, through Jesus Christ, man's lost dominion will one day be restored (Heb. 2:5–9).

—*Be Concerned*, pages 146–47

3. Review Zephaniah 1:1—2:4. What do you think it was like for Zephaniah to have to deliver the news about the upcoming Babylonian captivity? Would the people have believed him? Why or why not? If they did, how should that have changed their ways? How did they actually respond?

From the Commentary

The second picture of the day of the Lord is that of a *great sacrifice* (Zeph. 1:7–13). Since the Jewish people were accustomed to attending communal sacrifices (1 Sam. 9:11ff.), this image was familiar to them. But this sacrifice would be different, for it was God who was hosting the sacrifice. His guests were the Babylonians; and the sacrifices to be offered were the people of Judah! No wonder the prophet called for silence as he contemplated such an awesome event! (See Amos 6:10; 8:3; Hab. 2:20.)

You would expect the royal family and the religious leaders of the land to be the honored guests at God's feast, but they are the ones to be sacrificed (Zeph. 1:8–9)! God punishes them because they have abandoned His Word and adopted foreign practices, including wearing foreign clothes and worshipping foreign gods (see Num. 15:38; Deut. 22:11–12). After the death of King Josiah in 609 BC, the last four kings of Judah were weak men who yielded to the policies of the pro-Egyptian bloc in the government. Instead of trusting the Lord, they trusted their allies, and this led to disaster.

Zephaniah must have been a resident in Jerusalem, for he knew the layout of the city (Zeph. 1:10–13). When the Babylonians, God's guests, would come to the sacrificial feast, they would enter the city, plunder it, and then destroy it. The Fish Gate was where the fishermen had their markets; the "second quarter" was where the rich people lived in their fashionable houses, built from the

wages owed to poor laborers. "Maktesh" was the market
and business district of the city where the merchants and
bankers were located.

—Be Concerned, pages 147–48

4. Why was this prophecy so specific about how thoroughly the Babylonians
would do their work? How do you think the Israelites received this
threat? The tragedy could have been avoided if the people had listened to
Zephaniah and the other prophets. How would that have changed the Old
Testament story? Was the people's resistance to God's prophetic message
part of God's plan all along?

From the Commentary

God's judgment begins in the house of the Lord (1 Peter
4:17), which explains why Zephaniah started with the
people of Judah; but now he explains how the day of the
Lord will affect the Gentile nations surrounding Judah.
Though they were never given God's law as were the
Jews (Ps. 147:19–20), the Gentiles are still responsible
before God.... Furthermore, these nations had not always

treated the Jews kindly, and now the time had arrived for
God to judge them.

The nations named may represent all the Gentiles, since
these nations correspond to the four points of the com-
pass: Assyria (north), Cush (south), Moab and Ammon
(east), and Philistia (west). During the great day of the
Lord, all the nations of the earth will taste the judgment
of God.

—*Be Concerned*, page 150

5. Review Zephaniah 2:4–15. Why were the Gentiles still responsible before
God? (See Rom. 1:18–23.) What was the point of telling the Israelites the
fate of those surrounding Judah?

From the Commentary

Before we leave Zephaniah 1 and 2, we must note some
practical truths that apply to believers today. First, God
judges His people when they deliberately disobey His law.
His people are to be different from the other nations and
not imitate their ways or worship their gods (Num. 23:9;

Ex. 33:16; Deut. 32:8). "Be not conformed to this world" is an admonition for all believers today (Rom. 12:2; see 2 Cor. 6:14—7:1).

—*Be Concerned*, page 152

6. How did God judge His people in Zephaniah's time? How does He judge us today? Read Romans 12:2 and 2 Corinthians 6:14—7:1. In what ways are we expected to be different from nonbelievers?

From the Commentary

In Zephaniah 3, God reveals His plans for Jerusalem, the Gentile nations, and the faithful remnant. At the same time, the Lord reveals Himself and His gracious working on behalf of His people in every age and in every place.

Jerusalem is commonly called "the Holy City," but in Zephaniah's day, the city didn't manifest much holiness! Isaiah (1:21ff.), Jeremiah (29:12ff.), and Ezekiel (4—6, 9) gave the same assessment in their day. Even the Gentiles called Jerusalem "the rebellious and wicked city" (Ezra 4:12, 15 NIV), and they could cite proof for their statement.

Instead of being holy, the city was filthy and polluted because of shameful sin; and instead of bringing peace (*Jerusalem* means "city of peace"), the city was guilty of rebellion and oppression.

God expected the civil and religious leaders of the land to take His Word seriously and lead the people in the way of righteousness. Instead, the leaders acted like ravenous beasts in the way they oppressed the people and took what they wanted from them. The prophets were unfaithful to the Lord and His Word and dealt treacherously with the people. They didn't proclaim God's truth; they only preached what the people wanted to hear.

God's name was identified with the city and the temple (2 Sam. 7:13; 1 Kings 5:5; Neh. 1:9), and yet both were cesspools of iniquity. Therefore, He would have to act in judgment for His own name's sake. The wicked officials met at the city gate morning after morning to transact their evil business, and the Lord was there to behold their deeds. How patiently He waited, and yet they would not repent and turn to Him for cleansing!

—*Be Concerned*, pages 156–57

7. Review Zephaniah 3:1–8. What statements here could be said of corruption in our day? Do you think things are better today than what this passage describes? If so, in what ways? If not, why not? What can we do about corruption today? Explain.

From the Commentary

It's important to keep in mind that God's call of Abraham involved bringing God's blessing to the whole world (Gen. 12:1–3). God accomplished this by giving the Jews the knowledge of the true God, the written Word of God, and the Savior, Jesus Christ (Rom. 9:1–5). Therefore, they were to share these blessings with the Gentiles.

The Jews were supposed to magnify the Lord's name before the Gentiles. Instead, they imitated the pagan nations and disgraced God's name (Isa. 52:5; Rom. 2:24). The court of the Gentiles in the Jewish temple was supposed to be the place where Gentiles could talk with Jews about the true God and even pray to Him, but the religious leaders made that area into a market for selling sacrifices and exchanging money. What kind of testimony was that to the outsiders who were earnestly seeking the truth?

—*Be Concerned*, page 158

8. Review Zephaniah 3:9–10. What blessings does God promise for the Gentiles in the last days? Why is it significant in the larger scheme of God's plan for humanity that Zephaniah shared these prophecies about the Gentiles? How do you think these prophecies made the Israelites feel about their own specialness? What does this book of the Bible teach us about God's love for all people?

More to Consider: Read Isaiah 2:1–5; 4:1–6; and Zechariah 14:9–
21. (If you have time, also read Ezekiel 40—48.) What do these
verses teach us about the Gentiles' eventual response to God? How do
these passages help us see that the God of Israel is also the Lord of all
the earth? Does this minimize the unique relationship God has with
the Jews? Explain.

From the Commentary

When the terrible day of the Lord is over, Israel will be a
new nation. The Jews will look by faith upon the Messiah,
whom they crucified, believe in Him, and enter into a
new life in the promised kingdom.

The Jews won't have to be "put to shame" because when
they see Christ, they will be ashamed of what they did to
the Lord and will mourn over their transgressions (Zech.
12:10—13:1). It will be a time of deep repentance and
confession that will lead to salvation. God will especially
deal with the pride of Israel that for centuries had kept
them from submitting humbly to the righteousness of God
that comes only by faith in Christ (Rom. 9:30—10:13;
Phil. 3:1–12). There will be no place on God's holy hill for
proud sinners who think they can earn God's salvation by
their good works. In contrast to the proud sinners will be
the believing remnant, the "meek and humble, who trust
in the name of the LORD" (Zeph. 3:12 NIV).

—*Be Concerned*, page 159

9. Review Zephaniah 3:11–13. What does it mean in this passage that sin would be removed? How did Zephaniah's message suggest what was to come in the New Testament? How did God use His prophets to hint about the coming Messiah?

From the Commentary

During the seventy years of captivity in Babylon, and then during their worldwide dispersion among the Gentiles after AD 70, devout Jews were not able to celebrate their appointed feasts (Lev. 23). Since the destruction of the temple in AD 70, the Jewish people have had no temple, altar, priesthood, or sacrifice (Hos. 3:4–5). Of course, the types and symbols of the Old Testament law have all been fulfilled in Christ, including the feasts and sacrifices (Heb. 10), but Zephaniah intimates that these feasts will be restored in the kingdom age, and Zechariah 14:16–21 seems to support this interpretation.

—*Be Concerned*, page 161

10. Why would the Lord restore religious practices that have now been fulfilled? How is God's promise that His scattered people will be gathered a hopeful message (Zeph. 3:20)? How does this message also give us hope in today's church?

Looking Inward

Take a moment to reflect on all that you've explored thus far in this study of the book of Zephaniah. Review your notes and answers and think about how each of these things matters in your life today.

Tips for Small Groups: To get the most out of this section, form pairs or trios and have group members take turns answering these questions. Be honest and as open as you can in this discussion, but most of all, be encouraging and supportive of others. Be sensitive to those who are going through particularly difficult times and don't press for people to speak if they're uncomfortable doing so.

11. Zephaniah had to deliver some hard news to God's people. Describe a time when you had to share some tough news with someone you cared about. What role did your relationship with God play in how you delivered that news? How can your faith help you do such difficult tasks?

12. One of the common themes in this and all the books of the prophets is that of judgment. How would you have felt to hear God's judgment as the Israelites did time and time again? Do you ever feel judged by God? If so, why? How does grace change the rules of judgment?

13. While it's important to be present in this life, there's something to be said for looking ahead to what's to come. What are you most excited about regarding the coming kingdom of God? How can that hope help you live for Christ today?

Going Forward

14. Think of one or two things that you have learned that you'd like to work on in the coming week. Remember that this is all about quality, not quantity. It's better to work on one specific area of life and do it well than

to work on many and do poorly (or to be so overwhelmed that you simply don't try).

Do you want to have a humbler attitude? Be specific. Go back through the book of Zephaniah and put a star next to the phrase or verse that is most encouraging to you. Consider memorizing this verse.

Real-Life Application Ideas: The minor prophets had difficult jobs delivering often ominous news to an unwilling audience. But today the news we have to deliver to the world is good news! This week, be deliberate in sharing your faith with someone you've built a relationship with—or even a stranger, if you're comfortable with that. Trust God's guidance in how you approach this person, then be gracious and positive as you share exactly why the news of Jesus' life, death, and resurrection is the best news ever.

Seeking Help

15. Write a prayer below (or simply pray one in silence), inviting God to work on your mind and heart in those areas you've noted in the Going Forward section. Be honest about your desires and fears.

Notes for Small Groups:

- *Look for ways to put into practice the things you wrote in the Going Forward section. Talk with other group members about your ideas and commit to being accountable to one another.*
- *During the coming week, ask the Holy Spirit to continue to reveal truth to you from what you've read and studied.*

Summary and Review

Notes for Small Groups: This session is a summary and review of this book. Because of that, it is shorter than the previous lessons. If you are using this in a small-group setting, consider combining this lesson with a time of fellowship or a shared meal.

> *Before you begin ...*
> - *Pray for the Holy Spirit to reveal truth and wisdom as you go through this lesson.*
> - *Briefly review the notes you made in the previous sessions. You will refer back to previous sections throughout this bonus lesson.*

Looking Back

1. Over the past eight lessons, you've examined the books of Amos, Obadiah, Micah, and Zephaniah. What expectations did you bring to this study? In what ways were those expectations met?

2. What is the most significant personal discovery you've made from this study?

3. What surprised you most about the book of Amos? Obadiah? Micah? Zephaniah? What, if anything, troubled you?

Progress Report

4. Take a few moments to review the Going Forward sections of the previous lessons. How would you rate your progress for each of the things you chose to work on? What adjustments, if any, do you need to make to continue on the path toward spiritual maturity?

5. In what ways have you grown closer to Christ during this study? Take a moment to celebrate those things. Then think of areas where you feel you still need to grow and note those here. Make plans to revisit this study in a few weeks to review your growing faith.

Things to Pray About

6. Amos, Obadiah, Micah, and Zephaniah are ultimately books about God's plan for His people and the lengths that He goes to in enacting that plan. As you reflect on these books, thank God for the role each of these prophets played in preparing the world for Jesus' birth, life, death, and resurrection.

7. The messages in the books of Amos, Obadiah, Micah, and Zephaniah include judgment, promise, the coming kingdom, and hope for the future. Spend time praying for each of these topics.

8. Whether you've been studying this in a small group or on your own, there are many other Christians working through the very same issues you discovered when examining these prophetic books. Take time to pray for them, that God would reveal truth, that the Holy Spirit would guide you, and that each person might grow in spiritual maturity according to God's will.

A Blessing of Encouragement

Studying the Bible is one of the best ways to learn how to be more like Christ. Thanks for taking this step. In closing, let this blessing precede you and follow you into the next week while you continue to marinate in God's Word:

May God light your path to greater understanding as you review the truths found in the books of Amos, Obadiah, Micah, and Zephaniah and consider how they can help you grow closer to Christ.